Liza Coates £3

The Empty Bed

The Empty Bed

Bereavement
and the Loss of Love

SUSAN WALLBANK

Darton, Longman and Todd
London

First published in 1992 by
Darton, Longman and Todd Ltd
89 Lillie Road, London SW6 1UD

ISBN 0–232–51853–X

A catalogue record for this book is available
from the British Library

Cover: design by Sarah John

Phototypeset by Intype, London
Printed and bound in Great Britain
at the University Press, Cambridge

Contents

Contents

Introduction

When Bob had been dead for six weeks (remember he was taken ill and died all in one day) I woke in the night and momentarily forgetting, turned with love and need towards where he had lain; at first I felt some kind of guilt that while he was 'no more', I should be feeling desire. Later, I knew how well he would have understood that the habit of loving doesn't die or even diminish with separation. I listened to older friends who said things like: 'That's a side of life that is gone', or 'I don't miss that', or 'I'm glad that's over'. I kept silent because I felt so different. We had always said it was the best thing God ever thought up, and our desire was strong; even after thirty-five years together.

For women who do not enjoy physical love I have always felt pity, and, I'm afraid, a condemnatory feeling of criticism. So often they appear to be cheating or giving short measures of affection. Even when I was younger I learnt not to confide in other women in case I was dubbed as oversexed. Surely, if you love someone, it is the most natural way of expressing that love.

Over the past nine years I have found the loss of cuddling, kissing, hard to bear . . . leave alone making love. It sometimes seems so incredible that all my life, having enjoyed the warmth of physical contact, with first my parents, and then Bob, that I am now isolated in some refrigerator of iron-grey loneliness. It is akin to solitary confinement.

JEAN GAVE ME permission to use her letter, and I know she would not object if I described her as an 'older' woman. When she wrote those words she was in her seventies but

[1]

she still felt passionately about the physical loss she had suffered on the death of her husband, nearly a decade ago.

That 'refrigerator of iron-grey loneliness', which she describes, has never gone away – although an observer could look at Jean's life, and quite accurately define it as active, purposeful and full of excellent friendships.

For Jean, the sexual act is 'the most natural way of expressing love', but there are others who feel that our society places an unnatural overemphasis on sex, and, there are even those who believe that 'doing without it altogether' leaves us physically and mentally healthier and emotionally better adjusted.

Most of us choose to keep private the sexual side of our partnership, preferring not to confide in our friends or family. Perhaps like Jean, for fear of being seen as oversexed, or simply because we believe that what happens in 'that' part of our marriage is our business and ours alone.

Some people who lose a partner do feel a sense of relief when sexual demands are no longer placed upon them. Others may not go as far as that, but recognise that a natural ending has occurred; one that they can accept with dignity and resignation. There will also be those who, like Jean, privately cry out in frustration, longing to be held and loved once again. For anyone who has lost a partner, the reality of the empty bed lies at the end of each long day.

Sexuality is not just about making love. It is how we see ourselves as a man or as a woman. It is how we relate to other women and men around us. When the death of our partner takes us into the unknown world of loss and loneliness we will discover new sides to ourselves; new hopes, new fears and new desires. That process of change and discovery is challenging and exciting but it can also be a little frightening and the fear increases if there is no one around with whom we can talk; no one who understands what we are going through.

The bereaved person who wishes to talk about their sexual feelings, the young widow who has a problem concerning a male neighbour, the older widowed person searching for a way of making friends with members of the opposite sex, the widower contemplating remarriage – all may find themselves facing two major taboos; the taboo of death, and the taboo of sexuality. At a time when it would be most helpful to share hopes and dreams, doubts and fears, the door between them and the rest of the world swings shut.

Bereavement and sexuality make uneasy bedfellows. Bereavement asks us to look back and focus on the past, our sexuality locks us into the present, offering us the possibility of rebirth and new beginnings. Every step we take into our future takes us further from the one we have lost. Beginning again is never easy.

1

The Safety Net of Marriage

Our partner may be our husband or wife or our common-law spouse. Man or woman, they will be the person with whom we have chosen to live and build our future. Such partnerships are an agreement made between two adults based on choice; they are relationships of belonging to one another. We may not choose our family, our neighbours or working colleagues but, in our society, we can choose the person we wish to live with or marry.

Marriage is a legally binding, publicly acknowledged contract made between a man and a woman. The marriage-type partnership, formed between man and woman, or between woman and woman or man and man is not as firmly binding socially or legally but can, and often does, contain just as much love, companionship and long-term commitment and the pain and loss will be just as deep if it is ended by the death of one of the partners.

An increasing number of couples opt to live together before marriage. Not all will stay with that particular partner for ever, but if they do divorce or separate the odds are that, later, they will choose to live with someone again. The increase in the number of divorces and single-parent households in this country does not mean that marriage and the idea of long-term committed partnerships have gone out of fashion, far from it. Our society may have progressed and developed in the past few decades but it is still firmly based on the principle of the family and the pair. We continue to expect our young people to settle down with a partner of their choice, and most will do just that.

Although some relationships may ultimately be broken by separation or divorce, for the vast majority of couples entering marriage or cohabitation, the intention is that the union will last, either for ever or for a very long time indeed. Because of the length and security such partnerships offer, they are capable of containing a wide range of feelings; those of love, anger, irritation, respect and desire. Such contracts offer a continuity which allows time for change and development to take place within the relationship; a good partnership is a safe container for experiment and play. Partners learn each other's strengths and weaknesses; what brings a laugh, what causes pain. How best to avoid those dangerous areas that have to be negotiated with care if arguments are not to arise.

Marriage provides protection. It offers those within its contract an invisible safety net between them and the outside world. Any long-term, stable, pair relationship is capable of fulfilling a similar purpose.

As a society we are intensely curious about our fellow men and women. We like to know whether those we meet are married, single, divorced or widowed and it is quite likely that this information will be gained about a newcomer to the neighbourhood in a very short space of time. The majority of forms we are asked to complete will require this knowledge right at the very beginning. Individually and as a society we want to know the status and position of those around us. Having acquired this knowledge, it will play some part in how we act towards, and think about, our fellow men and women.

If we identify someone as part of a couple it is likely that we will behave in a certain way towards them. If we ask them to dinner we will probably include their partner in the invitation. Any flirtation might stop short of an actual proposal and, if a business deal is being conducted, it might be sensible to recognise that a partner may also have views on the subject.

Of course we never really *own* anyone or they us, but if we see ourselves as belonging to someone and they to us, this will change our concept of ourself. However liberated we may be within our personal contract; free to be ourselves and free to make our own decisions, at the back of our mind we carry with us the knowledge that we are one half of a partnership. We know that somebody cares for us; what affects us will affect them because of the union we have made.

There is all the difference in the world between being one of a couple and being a single person. Couples do things together: they dance together, go for a drink together, go home together at the end of an evening out. Couples can go on holiday together; they travel together and share memories of strange hotels in foreign lands. Couples cry together, laugh together and argue together. Couples are allowed to sleep together, they may not choose to but, if they do, it is alright. Sexuality is allowed between partners; one of the few acceptable outlets for it in our society.

Generally speaking couples make friends with other couples and ask other couples round for dinner. A couple may share not only friends, but property as well: a car, a home, possibly even a bank account. They share one another's families. They have mutual responsibility for, and pleasure in, any children they may have produced or brought with them into the union.

Couples may quarrel or adore each other; they may have times when they are angry, upset and irritated with one another. They may be madly in love or just a little bored. It does not matter, what does matter is the fact that they are part of an on-going, working, publicly acknowledged part-nership.

When living as part of a couple it is hard to appreciate the power and the privilege which goes with this position. Any one who has ever lost a partner through bereavement or divorce will have personal knowledge of the loss of status and security that follows such a major change.

Each marriage contains its own history; a beginning, a working middle period and an end. Few married people think towards that ending, they are naturally concerned with the actual business of life. Until illness or danger threatens it is unlikely that they will give serious consideration to the possibility that there will come a time when one or other of them may have to find a way of carrying on, partnerless and alone.

Most marriages include periods of difficulty and patches of serious confrontation mixed with the good times. It is not easy to live alongside another human being who has their own opinions, thoughts, needs, desires, wants and wishes. Sometimes these will match but, at other times, they will not, and then a compromise has to be reached. If major problems arise within the partnership, perhaps an affair or a temporary separation, it is possible that other members of the family and friends, even neighbours will get to know, but if the troubles resolve themselves they will sink into the background and become part of the history of the union.

Some marriages seem to have been made in heaven. The partners fit one another like a glove – emotionally, intellectually and sexually. Other rich and rewarding partnerships contain deep seated differences of interests or temperament. The partners not only agree to disagree but may positively benefit from the differences between them.

It is not at all unusual to have a difference in sexual needs within a marriage. This may reflect other aspects of the relationship or be a barometer of natural change. Over the years the balance of desire shifts as a couple passes from courtship, through the child-bearing and rearing years,

[7]

through midlife crises and menopause, and on into retirement and beyond.

What goes on within the privacy of the bedroom is rarely discussed with other people. It is the personal business between two consenting adults. It may be that both partners are sexually fulfilled, or that one is satisfied but the other unhappy, or that both feel there is room for improvement but can find no way of unlocking the patterns they have developed.

We can only guess at what takes place behind the closed curtains of a neighbour's bedroom. An attractive young wife may be coping with health problems that interrupt her ability to make love. An elderly couple with many slight disablements may have found a way to continue their satisfying love life. A couple may be making love once a night, once a week, once a year or not at all. Making love might include intercourse, oral sex or mutual masturbation. The range of what is considered normal sexual activity is very wide indeed.

Partners in a long-term relationship can acquire a tolerance and maturity of outlook which allows for differences of need and physical difficulties. The man may admire his beautiful, vivacious wife and re-enforce her public role as a sexual woman knowing secretly that she may have been frigid since the birth of their last child. Likewise a woman may support her good looking husband who flirts madly but harmlessly with all the young girls, knowing full well that he is impotent. A seemingly sterile relationship can conceal very high levels of sexual activity.

Couples protect one another. Their union allows them to play a certain part without fear of challenge from the outside world. As long as both partners are alive this protection continues. A sick or very ill partner will protect a well one. The very fact that there is a husband or wife somewhere in the background, even in hospital or a hospice, allows others to define us as part of a couple; this affects how they think about us and behave towards us. It will also influence their expectations of how we will behave towards them.

As long as we know that we are part of a couple our own sexual feelings can be safely contained within that union. If we have a very ill partner this may not be easy. The fact that they are ill and unable to make love does not instantly magic away our desires. Where there are long periods of separation we may already have explored ways of dealing with our frustration.

However, we are still protected; that safety net is still firmly in place. We are free at any time to say 'I am a married person. I do not want to do that!'

THE NET BREAKS

Once the safety net of marriage is removed anything can happen. Like Alice, falling down the well and finding herself in Wonderland, nothing quite makes sense any longer. The world the newly-bereaved widow or widower or partner (or divorcee) inhabits can be a strange place. We may find the behaviour of other people towards us unexpected and alarming. Yes, there is genuine kindness from friends but we may pick up other signals: 'surely that kiss was nearer the mouth that the cheek?' 'Surely we must have imagined Pat's reluctance to let John come over to repair our tap? She couldn't possibly think there could be anything going on – could she?'

We may also find ourselves thinking, feeling and acting in ways which surprise and disturb us. Partnerless, we stand alone, perhaps for the first time in our life. In the early days of their bereavement so many widows and widowers say: 'I feel only half a person, part of me has gone.' Without our partner there at our side we float, unanchored and undefined. We have lost our other half. For a while it can seem as if we have also lost ourselves. That person we used to be before the death has disappeared leaving us with this new bereaved self that we do not know.

Technically we have become a single person once again and yet never more than now are we attached to the one we have lost. Our thoughts are full of them and our bodies long for them. Every waking moment is filled one way or another with our exploration of that physical space that exists now between them and us. The passionate early days of being in love are very similar to the passionate, painful, early days of grief.

The loss of a partner affects our sense of security in so many ways. It can bring with it a sudden drop in status for to be part of a partnership can still confer a greater standing in our society than that afforded the single person. Even today a woman's central role in life may be at the heart of her family. Her authority and power in that family can be seriously threatened after the death of her husband when, deeply grieving, she is perceived as weak and vulnerable. Suddenly she may find herself being looked after and mothered by her own children.

The centre of the family may shift away from the old family home to one of the new units created by the children. The older widow or widower may find their role within the family diminished by the death of their partner. Where once their word was respected, their opinion sought, now they may feel isolated – seen as a problem to be dealt with by younger family members.

Some people acquire status and position in the community through their partner's job; the wives and husbands of doctors, vicars, company managers, politicians and many small business owners often have a very active and important part to play in their spouse's work, and death can suddenly strip this role away. The position of one partner in society may give the other access to a world which they would never have entered if he and she had not been joined together in a partnership. The death of one may leave the other outside the security of that magic inner circle.

Very often partners are also best friends. Indeed, that may well have been the reason why we became partners. The deep friendship and ease of companionship may have grown and developed over the years. Best friends know what we were about to say, even before the words had left our lips. Best friends are often the only people we can really relax with; sharing a laugh or a sadness with equal ease. When a best friend dies that deep friendship dies with them. Who will we relax with now that our best friend has gone?

Our partner may be a parent to our children. They share with us the burdens and the pleasures of family life, caring as much as we do. When our partner dies we are left to be both mother and father to our children. We become one of the many thousands of single parents attempting to give their children the love, discipline and security they need to grow up strong and healthy.

There may be other family responsibilities we shared with our partner; the care of a mentally sick aunt or a disabled parent. As long as the burden was carried by two people, it was bearable. What happens now when there is only one grieving person left to take the strain?

All partnerships have a financial basis and it is likely that our partner's earnings contributed to the running of the household, either as the main or a supplementary income. When they die we lose not just our partner, but the financial security they provided: their salary, wages, pension, benefit, or secondary income may have formed a vital part of the weekly budget, providing, if not the necessities, then some of the nonessential luxuries which make such a difference to the quality of life. Our partner may have handled the finances of the household and we may have to learn how to do this. How will the bills be paid? What about the funeral? Can I afford a holiday this year, or ever again? How much tax should I be paying, if any?

When living in a partnership it makes good sense to pool resources. It is not necessary that both partners need to know everything; most couples distribute the various household tasks reasonably fairly. The system works well until one of the partners dies. When we lose a partner all the skills they possess die too; skills that may have to be replaced one way or another if we are to survive.

Our partner may have been the one who drove the car, and without them we find ourselves living out of reach of clubs, supermarket, friends and relatives. Public transport may be unreliable, or even nonexistent, and the world dwindles abruptly to a street or two, and the corner shop. Should we learn to drive or should we move home? Can we afford a taxi once a week or rely on the help of good friends and neighbours?

Our partner may have been the gardener, and we are faced with a wilderness of weeds, a lawn that seems to need constant mowing, hedges that grow overnight. When do you prune a rose? Would it be better to pave the flower beds? How much does a gardener cost?

Our partner did all the cooking. How are we to feed ourselves now they have gone? They were the housekeeper, they changed the sheets and did the washing each week and vacuumed the living room and scrubbed the kitchen floor. How does the washing machine work? What programme should be used for blankets?

Our partner did all the house maintenance and decoration. How do you fix a shelf to a wall? How do you safely wire up a plug? Do you always have to apply an undercoat first before painting a window frame? How on earth does the central heating system work? Why didn't I find out when there was still time?

Our partner was the one who remembered the family birthdays. The knowledge of these was kept in their head and no record now exists. It is hard to say to a very close relative, 'I'm afraid I don't know the date of your birthday'. Our partner may have been the present buyer; they knew what people wanted for Christmas. Do five-year-old children still read books? Would Uncle Ted like a record token? Our partner may have been the one who removed the spider from the bath; the one who climbed the ladder to fix that awkward light bulb; the one who locked the house up safely each night. How can we ever feel safe at night again now they are no longer here?

Few areas of life remain unaffected after the loss of a partner. We may lose our health for a while for such a major bereavement can produce physical symptoms, especially in the early weeks and months of grief. The stress and tension of the early days of mourning can deplete our precious reserves of energy, leaving us to fall prey to every virus and germ we come into contact with. Old illnesses may flare up once more. From defining ourselves as a healthy person we may begin to see ourselves as fragile and vulnerable.

A good night's sleep can become a luxury after a partner's death. So often sleep is disturbed at this time and the nights contain long hours when there is no defence against the sadness, no distraction from the pain of loss. The rest of the world lies peacefully slumbering while we lie here, staring at the ceiling. There is no one to telephone, no one to communicate with. The morning will provide no relief; we wake to a world dominated by loss, sadness and sheer exhaustion.

We may lose concentration at the very time when we need to think hard and fast. There can be so much work to be done after the death of a partner; papers to be found, people to be contacted, telephone calls to make, forms to fill in, endless decisions to be made. Memory can be affected. We arrive at the shops forgetting what we wanted to buy. We find ourself forgetting names, forgetting what day of the week it is. We may even forget what the dead person looked like before they became ill, forget the things they said and did, how they laughed or smiled. The feeling that we will never remember things again; that they have slipped away into the black hole of the past, can be very frightening indeed.

Bereavement causes us to lose control over so much of our life. It can affect us emotionally and physically. Tears come when we least want them – on the top of the bus or in front of a child and then, confusingly, refuse to flow when we are alone and feel so full of sadness; the anger that suddenly flashes; the panic attacks; the trembling; the sighing; we may find ourselves not wanting to eat, or, conversely, eating non-stop; we discover ourselves on spending sprees we can ill afford, or consuming that second or third alcoholic drink before bedtime.

Many people who lose a partner speak with sadness of the loss of some of their long-term friendships. Relationships which are not strong enough to survive the change and disruption bereavement brings with it. These are the unexpected, unprepared-for losses. Eventually they may be balanced out by the creation of new friendships more in keeping with our new position in life.

The death of our partner will change how we live. Its repercussions will only slowly be discovered in the months following our loss. The habit patterns and structures that underlie each day will all be affected. From the moment of waking to the moment we try to sleep, everything is changed because there is no partner now at our side; no one to eat with, talk with, sleep with. No one to wait for at the end of the working day. Sometimes we forget; we put two plates on the table instead of one, buy a packet of sugar when no one takes it anymore.

Many of those losses will not last for ever. We will, in time, sort out our financial affairs and find a way of coping within our new income level. Slowly we may find that we can sleep again at night although perhaps never quite as we did once. We may begin to feel a great deal stronger physically as the months pass and we may even get used to living alone. People do. Some even begin to quite like the sense of independence that solo living gives.

Many aspects of loss can be talked over with kind friends, our parish priest or minister, or a sympathetic doctor. People will try and understand, they may also, in time begin to suggest possible solutions to some of the many difficulties we face; there may be no shortage of good advice. In time we will become expert problem solvers. However, it is very likely that our partner will also be our lover – our sexual partner – and this is a loss that will rarely be spoken of. It is probable that as a bereaved person we will not be assumed to be missing our partner physically and sexually. Of course we will. Every night we enter the empty bedroom and stare down at the empty bed. There is no one there now to cuddle close to, no one to hug or kiss good night. Every night we will be faced with the likelihood that this part of our life has ended – for ever.

A bereaved partner faces not just the loss of the satisfaction that accompanies making love with their partner – the person they love. The loss extends far beyond the receiving and giving of immediate pleasure. It is also the loss of being told, 'you are beautiful'. It is the loss of being wanted and found desirable. It is the loss of being seen as a complete woman or a total man.

It can be through our partner that we have access to the world of the opposite sex. Having a wife allows a man an intimate glimpse into womanhood. Having a husband enables a woman to understand what it is to be a man. The loss of a partner can close that door. It is all too easy to be caught in a single sex system. However much we may enjoy the company of our own sex we will still long, not just for our man or our woman, but for that door between us and the opposite sex to be opened once again. This aspect of our loss often remains silent and unspoken; it is not easily understood by friends or family. Against all the other losses it may seem small, even insignificant in the numbing and bewildering early days of bereavement. But it is a loss that at times may appear overwhelming.

It can be painful to feel that we have become sexually redundant; that those special skills are no longer needed. For there are great skills involved in making love, and in loving and being loved. This loss of identity as a sexual being joins with all those hundreds and thousands of other losses that follow the death of a beloved partner.

Even in the darkest early days of grief we search for a ray of hope, for a glimpse of a future which is not totally black. It can be hard, even impossible, to focus on anything positive when there is so much loss. At such a time all we can do is live one day at a time, mourn for all that has gone for ever from our lives, and wait.

2

Different Love – Different Loss

There is much that forms a common bond between all who lose a beloved life partner but how we grieve, how our life will be actually altered and changed by that bereavement, will depend upon a multitude of other influences. No two partnerships are the same and death may strike at any point in the history of a union. Whether we are a man or a woman will also play a part in the way we view life after our bereavement. The widow will confront problems not experienced by the widower, for to be a man alone is not the same as to be on one's own as a woman. Our age also matters. The young girl who loses her boyfriend will not be facing exactly the same problems as the elderly man on the death of his wife. The ending of the relatively new relationship creates a different kind of loss to that generated by the ending of a relationship which has lasted many decades. There will be particular aspects of the loss experienced by the man and woman who loses their partner in the middle years of their life or for those who are left to care alone for young children.

When a group of bereaved partners meet together for the first time they often begin by exploring the differences that exist between them. The women envy the men their ability to travel alone without fear. The men will express the wish that they had close friends like the women. The young widow who feels she has lost her future envies the older woman the time she had with her husband before his death. The older man may wonder why the younger man grieves so deeply for the ending of so brief a relationship. As group members get to know one another the similarities emerge; the practical problems, the loneliness and sense of isolation that can dominate the lives of all who have lost a beloved partner. Before we look more closely at these shared experiences and the process of grief itself we will explore some of the differences.

Not all partnerships are neatly contained inside the clearly defined boundary of the marriage contract. An increasing number of people are choosing to live together either as a prelude to their eventual marriage or because they have no wish to convert their relationship into a marriage.

YOUNG LOVE

There are the young who lose a lover or a fiancé; those intense relationships which have not reached the altar or the registry office before they are prematurely ended by death. Committed, caring unions which contain the intention that they will last for ever, a wish which is dramatically curtailed.

No one ever expects to lose a young lover through death. Death is for the old not for the young, and yet, sadly, young people do die. They are involved in road accidents or other violent unexpected happenings. The young are still learning, they are adventurous and therefore they are at risk. And youth does not give immunity from illness and disease, the young can and do become sick and sometimes that sickness is fatal. The young are emotional and idealistic. Very occasionally a young person feels that their existence is unbearable and they take their own life.

The death of a young person who should have the world ahead of them is seen by society as a tragedy and it will have a tragic and profound effect on the lives of many people. This is reflected in the size of the funeral as relatives, friends and colleagues gather together to mourn their loss.

Where does the boy or girlfriend of the deceased fit into such a situation? Much will depend on the length of the relationship and its acceptance as a permanent union by those closest to the couple. If there has been no formal engagement, no public acceptance of it, then it is possible that the young lover will be placed into a category only slightly above that of friendship. The very special relationship they shared, which may have included physical closeness may go virtually unacknowledged by other people. Compared with a parent's loss of a child, the boy or girlfriend's loss may seem almost insignificant. It will not be insignificant to the young lover. For him or her the world has changed for ever. This may be the first time they have faced a bereavement, their first confrontation with death. Now they stand on the edge of an alien land overwhelmed by changing and intense emotions.

For people in love the length of their relationship in terms of weeks or months has little or no meaning. Once that decision to love has been made it is the present and the future which become all important. When such an affair is ended abruptly by death, it can seem as if love itself has died. How hard it can be to grapple alone with the concept that the flesh that has been a part of us is now dead; that the mouth that voiced words of love is silenced for ever; that a person, so recently full of life, should have no life left to live.

This silent and unacknowledged grief is different from the publicly recognised loss; the love affair which is accepted by relatives and friends and which allows for the public expression of grief. A young girlfriend may become very close to her boyfriend's parents as they mourn together the loss they have suffered. A sharing of love and affection for the one who has died may bring the two generations mutual comfort.

One of the great difficulties in losing someone we love by

death when we are young is the fact that it is unlikely we will meet anyone else in exactly our situation. There may be no one around with whom we can share thoughts and discuss feelings. It is through such a process that we are able to work out what might be normal and what is definitely abnormal behaviour and emotions!

When we are young everything is for ever. Love is for ever and when it ends it ends for ever. It follows that we are bereaved for ever and that the pain will go on for ever. If we become depressed, that too will last for ever. This ignores that major lesson that death teaches us which is that nothing, even life itself, can be for ever. This pain, this sadness, this grief and loneliness, this too will pass.

How long does grief last? It can be assumed by those around us that we should get over it in a matter of weeks or months; that we are ready to make new relationships when we are far from that stage. Some religions have a defined period of mourning but all too often there is no prescribed recipe for mourning. This means that there is every opportunity to get it wrong, to act badly or inappropriately. 'For goodness sake! She died last summer and you're still moaning around the place like a wet blanket', is one response. The other might be: 'He's hardly cold in his grave and you out with another boy. I don't think it's right'.

With no set rules how do we know when it is right to start a new relationship? There is no easy answer to that question. What feels right to one person may appear all wrong to another. All we can do is listen to what our feelings are telling us and to other people's thoughts and opinions and remember that, ultimately the responsibility for the decisions we make remains with us and us alone.

COHABITATION

An increasing number of people are now choosing to cohabit. Many of these common law unions are marriages in all but name; two people living together as a couple, sharing property and perhaps a common responsibility for the care of children. When death terminates such a partnership the one who is left will share all the tribulations, the grief, the problems of their widowed brother or sister and perhaps one or two additional difficulties as well.

The longer the partnership, the more possessions held in common, the easier it may be for others to recognise and acknowledge the loss. The most important and precious of these shared responsibilities will, of course, be any children coming from the union. Children from previous unions will also be deeply affected by the death of a much loved parent figure.

Widows and widowers have clear legal rights, those who cohabit do not. Many who lose an unmarried partner discover this fact to their cost. At a time of shock they find themselves having to deal with difficult practical matters, which, if unresolved could present a real threat to the whole basis of their future security. If they shared a home they must establish their right to remain there after the death. If there is any dispute over a tenancy agreement or ownership of the property then legal advice should be sought as soon as possible. A deceased partner's relatives may feel that they have a claim to all or part of the inheritance. The more loosely defined the relationship, the more danger of disputes arising if it is ended prematurely in death.

The less defined the relationship, the harder it can be to mourn its passing. We may receive less support from our friends and family who have only a very hazy picture of the loss we have suffered and the depth of sadness we feel. We may also feel confused as to how we should be feeling and acting. The words which describe a form of bereavement, such as widow or orphan can be useful as they produce a mental picture of a grieving person or child. If we have no words to describe clearly the relationship which existed between us and the one we have lost, it can be hard to convey the full extent of the pain and grief we are feeling.

Just as our society is searching for new laws and contracts to secure these important relationships, so perhaps we also need to find new words to describe them. Boyfriend and girlfriend seem hardly appropriate once past a certain age. Such relationships extend beyond being mere lovers, and common law husband and wife seem clumsy titles which as yet have not been extended to common law widow or widower. However, those in committed, long-term unions will face many of the problems confronted by the widowed. Much which is written in this book for the widowed will apply equally to a relationship based on a common law partnership.

EX-WIVES AND HUSBANDS

Some relationships span the years, are of immense importance to the participants but remain virtually hidden from the world. A man may love his ex-wife, a woman her ex-husband, in such a way. The marriage broke down decades ago, both halves of the couple may have married again, found new partners, new lovers, but the feelings go on and on. Ex-husbands and ex-wives may be deeply affected by the death of their ex-partner. When a partnership has once contained great physical and mental closeness, we can never quite dismiss it from our minds. It is part of our history and we are the product of that history. To lose part of our history is to lose part of ourselves.

When we mourn the loss of a relationship, the usual assumption is that we will mourn the most recent part, that which has just passed. It is because of this belief that there can be puzzlement at someone who expresses great sadness following the death of someone they may have had very little contact with for many years. Why should we need to mourn the loss of someone who has so little importance in our day-to-day lives?

Our ability to grieve is not locked into a time-scale. The news of the death of someone we once loved can bring deep sadness. Our mind turns back to the past and we may remember scenes that have lain hidden for years. Those scenes may contain passionate early love. We grieve for the loss of that person who once loved us so much. We may grieve too for other associated losses, the loss of our beauty and youth as we compare the young person we once used to be with our present self. Such a death can have great significance for us and enable us to reassess our present and our future because of the knowledge we gain from investigation of our past.

LOVERS

Mistresses and lovers can find it hard to find a way of openly expressing their sadness. Often such relationships are secret or unacknowledged by those around them.

A mistress or a lover may have no right to attend the funeral, or even to receive knowledge of the death of his or her lover. If they are fortunate they will be accepted as a friend of the deceased and this will give some opportunity to grieve openly and take part in the proceedings surrounding the death. If there was no open friendship then feelings may have to be carefully contained for, if it was felt necessary to maintain secrecy when both partners were alive, the reasons that led to that decision being taken then will probably still remain after the death.

This places a strain on the grieving person. His or her loss is great and yet there may be no one with whom they can pour out their pain and distress. Perhaps this is a time when the confidentiality of counselling is most important as it allows feelings to be expressed with no danger that they will be fed back to those who may find them damaging.

Sexual intercourse may have played a very large part in such a relationship, especially at the beginning, but besides sex there may have been humour and love and a lifetime commitment between the couple, an understanding that the relationship between the two of them was intended to stretch far into the future.

It is all too easy to underestimate the importance of these secret loves. Many may have ceased to be actively sexual but they brought sexuality into the lives of those that loved. When they end the sense of barrenness and sterility can be hard to overcome. It is as if all the joy has gone from life for ever.

HOMOSEXUAL PARTNERS

Two people meet, fall in love and decide to set up home together. They live together for many years and then one of them dies. The surviving partner may have no rights to arrange the funeral or to lay claim to the property of the deceased in spite of the length and importance of the relationship that has been ended by death. The grief and sadness of the surviving partner may be ignored by relatives of the one who has died and possibly by friends and colleagues at work. They may find that their presence is unwelcome at the funeral. A partner has died, a major bereavement has taken place and no one appears to notice or care.

Such an intense distressing situation is most likely to happen if those two people who loved one another were of the same sex. The bereaved homosexual lover will face all the problems and painful feelings experienced by a widow or widower who loses a partner through death, but, alongside their need to grieve and their need to create a new existence, there may be other unexpected and distressing difficulties.

They may find themselves particularly isolated and alone. All grief can isolate and loneliness is so much a part of life after the death of a partner; but the grief of the man or woman who loses their gay lover may not be fully recognised or acknowledged by those around; perhaps due to embarrassment, that not-knowing-what-to-say syndrome which is exacerbated if the relationship is not clearly defined. The bereaved gay partner may find it very hard indeed to meet others who could really appreciate the loss they have suffered.

The multitude of loss a homosexual or lesbian faces will range from that of a sexual partner through to loss of companionship and on to the loss of a mutual homemaker. There may also be loss of financial security if the deceased was the main wage earner. All this loss may be packaged by society into the simple loss of a friend.

And what of the future? In the early days of grief this can appear very bleak indeed. That which has been lost can never be replaced and the chances of finding such a love a second time might be only a remote possibility. The task of rebuilding life after so much of its meaning and purpose has been destroyed can seem a daunting one indeed.

It is not always easy for homosexuals to get to know other homosexuals. The majority live quiet, contained lives with their partners. Few gay bars or clubs exist outside the major cities and it can take courage to attend such gatherings, the kind of courage that is simply not there in the early days of loss. Many would find such gatherings inappropriate.

There may be times when the need to lay down solid foundations for the future seem directly at odds with the body's need for love and sexual satisfaction. So often one half of ourselves seems to be fighting the other after a major bereavement. Those inward-looking needs of grief conflict with the outward task of restructuring a social life capable of enabling us to avoid isolation. The ending of any partnership containing a close physical relationship will bring us sadness and pain. We may have to come to terms with sexual feelings which have no clear outlet. The consequences of such a loss may leave us feeling lost and very alone.

Over the past few years, the link between homosexuality and Aids has presented an unbalanced picture of men who choose to love other men. However, for those who might have lost a lover through this terrible disease the two themes of this book, bereavement and sexuality, are intertwined in a particularly poignant way. For them, death and sexuality have become permanently linked together; that which has brought most joy and satisfaction to life is also the bringer of the greatest pain and loss.

The threat of contracting Aids is a real fear for homosexual men seeking new sexual partners (it is one that should not be ignored by heterosexual lovers either). Never more than in our present society has there been a need for honesty in the formation of new unions.

The gay man and the lesbian woman may find themselves particularly alone after the death of their partner. The full extent of the loss they have suffered may pass unrecognised by those around them.

THE YOUNG WIDOW AND WIDOWER

No one expects to be widowed in their twenties, their thirties or even their early forties. When making their marriage vows most people do so in the belief that only death will divide them and that such a parting by death will be a long way off in the future. After all, people are living longer nowadays. Most young people have at least one grandparent still alive and, it is not unreasonable to assume that partners will live on until they are in their seventies, if not their eighties.

No one expects death to interrupt the early, often hard working years of marriage. These can be a period containing financial and emotional pressures when the foundations for the future are gradually established. A home has to be created. The marriage has to be protected and looked after. Other people are involved because the marriage union is also a union of two families. These may be years of exploration, self-discovery and change. This period often involves the making of major decisions; the giving up of economic gain for the sake of the future, delaying having much wanted children until there is a degree of financial security. Such decisions are made on the assumption that there are still years ahead to become pregnant, and bring up children; decades of love and comradeship still to come.

The loss of a partner at a young age is the disruption of the present and the loss of the future. Death brutally and abruptly cuts existence in half. There can be a sense of out-rage and anger at the unfairness of it all. 'Why me? Why has my life been destroyed?'

The young generally lose young partners and the young do not die easily. It takes disaster, accident, suicide or a virulent disease to break the grip that a young man or woman has on life. The death of a young person is more likely to be a sudden death or one following a severe illness. Conse-quently the transition from young wife to young widow, young husband to young widower, is likely to be a sudden or a painful one.

Because it is still relatively rare to lose a partner at an early stage the young widow or widower may feel an even greater sense of isolation. The only other single people they meet are likely to be still married or separated or divorced from their partners. The feelings of a young divorcee towards the opposite sex may be very different indeed to those of the young widow or widower. In the early months of bereavement, in many ways, people are 'in love' with the person they have lost. Unlike the divorced man or woman, it is unlikely that they will be angry with all men or all women. After all, the one they have lost, the person they love most was a member of the opposite sex and with him or her they have lost access to that other world.

It is possible that this may also be the first major bereavement faced by friends and family. No one will know quite what to say or how to act in this very new and distressing situation. People may attempt to offer comfort, giving assurance that they understand what it must be like to lose someone. How could anyone understand such a shocking and impossible event? Comforting remarks may include 'You're young, you'll marry again.' When all they want is their partner back there is little comfort in the thought of a replacement. Yet the alternative, the thought of facing a lifetime, perhaps fifty years alone, unloved, untouched, unwanted by anyone is an unbearably painful prospect.

'Why don't you come home?' The very young widow or widower can find that, as far as parents are concerned, their real home is still with them and they are encouraged to give up their present flat or house. There may be a lot of sense in going back home for a while; in taking the opportunity to be mothered and comforted and looked after. In the early days of bereavement it may be painful to stay in their own house or flat where every object can seem to bring with it a reminder of the loss that has been suffered; painful to wake alone, to go to sleep alone and live surrounded by memories from the past. However, the prospect of returning to their parental home can also bring with it the fear that they will slip back into the past, become a child once more and that everything that has been created with their partner will disappear for ever.

In an attempt to help, relatives and friends may suggest we should think about the future. Better to put the past behind us, it only brings pain to dwell on the sadness; better to forget it, better not to even mention his or her name. The younger we are, the shorter the length of the relationship shared with the deceased, the more vulnerable we will be to this kind of comforting advice. The younger we are, the less capable other relatives may feel we are of making funeral arrangements or taking charge of other practical matters such as the settlement of the estate. Our short relationship, even if it was technically a partnership, may not appear to carry the same weight of loss as that suffered by another who knew the deceased longer. In many cases there is a clear 'main' griever, a person who quite obviously is the one who has lost most by a death. However, in other cases this is not clearly defined. A mother of a dead daughter may feel that her loss is far greater than that suffered by a very young husband although she might sympathise with his sadness.

An increasing number of young couples find themselves living far from their original home towns. The bonds between young people and their families grow fragile and when trouble comes there is no family to turn to for love and support, no relatives to offer advice and practical help. When one partner dies the remaining one can find themselves facing their grief very much alone.

Young partners may be still in love with one another and make love regularly. Death brings that loving relationship to an end. Now, a thousand years later, they climb into the empty double bed and wonder if this is what it will be like for ever? Women wonder if they should carry on taking the contraceptive pills until the pack is finished, or if they should arrange to have the coil removed. After all, such precautions are not necessary any more. There is no need for any kind of birth control now.

Perhaps it would be sensible to keep on the pill, just for a while. To keep the coil in, just in case? In case of what? There is nothing in life now which does not seem to require the necessity of making a decision and the last thing a woman may feel like at this time is making any decision however large or small. The removal of the coil can be yet another ending, one that may appear to herald the finish of sexuality, the final end to being a woman. Of course this is not so. The fact that a woman may not be making love at this very moment does not mean that she has ceased to be a woman, she most definitely is! She is a woman who is grieving deeply for the loss of her mate, her man.

It is possible that the shock of bereavement may affect a woman's monthly periods. Some women find that these are interrupted for a time, others suffer from irregular or heavy periods for the first few months. Women who have started the menopause may find that they start to bleed again, perhaps their first period for over a year. Others discover that the loss of their husband coincides with their menopause and that they thus confront two endings at the same time.

Being a widower – what does that mean? What rules govern the behaviour of a young widower? How is he expected to behave? Widows often envy the freedom that their male counterparts seem to have. 'You can go into a pub for a drink. We can't!' they might say. In vain men assure women that not all of them like spending every night of the week in a pub. They didn't marry to be in the company of men; they married a woman. They wanted to spend their evenings with that woman. At night they wanted to go to bed with that woman. They still do. The problem is that she is dead. Now there is no one to talk to after work. They are alone.

Although male friends may prove supportive both during a long illness and after death, providing a much needed sense of identity and comradeship, some men do find it hard to dwell on sadness or discuss feelings in depth with other men. It is often with women that men are best able to open up and admit their sadness and vulnerability. The one person they are used to sharing such feelings with is no longer there.

Many men will simply contain their emotions and get on with the task of survival. Trained to act like a man; told since they were little that big boys don't cry, they may be congratulated on their strength by doctors and relatives.

They may have promised their wife that they would be brave, perhaps for the sake of the children.

'I feel just like a little child.' One man confided after his wife's death and the loss of someone we love deeply does indeed make us feel as exposed and vulnerable as a child. We long to be held, we long for someone to make everything alright again. We want the pain to go away. In a good partnership we can be everything to our mate and they can be our lover, our child and our parent. When they leave the loss is enormous. There is no friend, no lover and no mate. No mothering or fathering arms to hold us tight and take away the pain and the fear.

One young widower described what he needed just six months after his wife had died leaving him with a toddler and a small baby to bring up: 'a brothel with a creche!' Many other single fathers might echo that cry but recognise its impossibility. If one accepts the creche-type support necessary to care for a young family then this will usually preclude the brothel facilities. Any strange young woman visiting a single man's home will very quickly be spotted and remarked upon by the neighbours. Suddenly he will find himself without Mrs Jones' help in picking up the toddler from nursery school and Mrs Smith might not seem quite so willing to babysit in future.

Of course, not all young widowers will be looking for sexual encounters in the early months of their bereavement. Each man is an individual following his own unique pathway through the pain and sadness which is a consequence of the death of his wife. For some men the thought of sleeping with another woman at such a time would be untenable. Numbed by the appalling loss he has suffered his concentration will be on survival and getting through each endless day.

Women generally outlive their partners, so men tend to have a higher expectation that they will go first and the death of a wife at any age can seem a cruel twist of fate. Perhaps in the days when it was not unusual to lose a wife in child-birth the blow of death was not totally unexpected. But today's society does not expect to lose its young people at the very age when they are beginning to create their own family units and embark on the huge task of parenting the next generation.

In spite of women's rights and an increased awareness of the benefits of sharing family roles, not a great deal has changed in the distribution of tasks within a family. On the whole men will still go out to work and the expectation in most relationships is that they will continue to do so whilst, at some time, a woman will stop work for a while to give birth to their child or children.

It is generally the wife who cares for the running of the house, is mainly in charge of the cooking and the shopping and the washing. A wife is usually the partner who sends out the birthday cards and creates those important little links with the various sides of the family. This is not to say that men do not contribute in all these tasks, many do, but most households are, by necessity, run on a system of division of labour. It is simply more efficient to do so.

When there is no wife there to ensure that the family is kept united and the house cleaned and cared for, it is all too easy for the young widower to find himself isolated and living in a state of chaos. There are only so many hours in the day. How is it possible to combine the demands of full-time work and learn a whole set of new skills and routines at a time when he is grieving deeply for all that has gone from life for ever?

Many men are highly skilled problem solvers. When confronting a crisis in life which is creating problems emotionally and practically, it seems logical to seek out a solution. If they are lonely and alone and if they love women and had a good marriage and if they need someone to care for their home and if they have young children who need a mother it might seem logical to search for a new partner. This would appear the ideal solution to all their difficulties in life. More widowers than widows remarry and their marriages take place sooner after the death of their wife than the marriages formed by their female counterparts. Sadly, not all second marriages are successful. People take their history with them into these new beginnings; memories, past love, home, failures and successes, children, in-laws and family travel with them into the future. The success of that future is based on the ability to have dealt successfully with the past.

Young widows and widowers may be inundated with, often conflicting, advice and recommendations. 'Get out more, join something, it will do you good!' 'You don't want to be rushing about, give yourself time to grieve!' 'I think it's a bit soon to be going to a party.' Widows and widowers of all ages find themselves in a no-win situation. If they go out they are considered unfeeling and forward, if they don't they are considered morbid and introspective.

Caught between the demands of the past and the hopes for the future; between our own needs, if only we knew what they were, and the expectations of others, being widowed confronts us with a multitude of problems and, in the early days of our loss, precious few clear solutions.

THE MIDDLE YEARS

There is no right or good time to lose a beloved partner and become single once again. Each age contains its own particular and unique set of difficulties.

What is middle age and when does it occur? Unlike the teens or senior citizenship it is not easy to define. It lies somewhere between forty and sixty. For a woman it contains the menopause, that physical expression of the end of the child-bearing era. It is some time in these two decades that children form their own families and leave home. It can be a time when a married couple will begin tentatively to think about their future and perhaps start planning for retirement. It may be a time when couples begin to draw closer together, freeing themselves at last from the pressure and strain that adolescents and late teenagers can place on a relationship. The roles of mother and father become a little less important as there is less mothering and fathering to be done. The roles of husband and wife begin to dominate once again.

At any age the death of a partner brings with it a loss of meaning and purpose but, when this is combined with the dilution of the role as parent, the sense of emptiness can seem overwhelming. This can be a particularly cruel time to lose half of oneself. Friends, fortunate to have their partners, continue to pursue their normal lives; meeting together in couples, planning their futures, beginning to reap the rewards of decades of hard work. For the widowed person there is to be no such reward and there can be a sense of being cheated of his or her rightful future. Middle-aged people are often balanced somewhere in the middle of two generations. The pull of the younger, the children, may be lessening but against this the older generation, the parents, may exert an increasing need for care and attention.

It is worth holding on to the thought that the very factor that increases loneliness at this period, the easing away of the responsibilities of children, also gives the middle-aged widow or widower the freedom to create new friendships and make decisions about the future knowing they are free to do so without obligation.

The middle-aged person often feels there is no place for them in society. They are too old for the associations, the discos and clubs for the young and single person, and too young for those designated as suitable for the senior citizen. Nothing seems to offer the middle-aged man or woman a proper sense of identification. It is as if they float shapeless and unobserved in the twilight zone between youth and old age!

When a man or woman is grieving deeply, when their

sleep is disturbed and their face drawn and lined with sadness and distress it can be difficult to hold onto the idea of themselves as beautiful or desirable. In the middle years the death of a partner can seem like the death of youth. Desperately the grieving middle-aged widow stares into the mirror at a face that only yesterday was young and tries to hold onto the fact that she is still an attractive and possibly desirable woman. The widower inspects his thinning head of hair and sighs. There can be no hiding such visible signs of ageing.

Perhaps one of the positive contributions made by the media to our society in the past decade is the explosion of the myth that a woman is 'past it' at forty. There are simply too many beautiful older women on our screens for that statement to be accepted any longer. In fact, there is increasing evidence that women mature far later than men and may be approaching their physical prime towards the end of their thirties. With careful use of hormone therapy when necessary there is no longer the need for a woman to be a martyr to her body throughout her menopause. When this is at last completed, released from the threat of unwanted pregnancy, women often feel fitter and healthier and more attractive than they have for many a year.

How can such thoughts help the woman who stares into her mirror and sees reflected there the pale face of a grieving widow? They may give reassurance that the end of the sexual and loving relationship she had with her husband is not synonymous with the end of herself as a sexual person. She is still a woman. She may choose never to make love with another man but that choice will not make her less a woman. The path ahead of her does not lead her ever downward into frustration, ugliness and eventual death. Far from it. She will grow stronger. It is quite possible that men may find her attractive again. It is possible that already she has discovered to her confusion that they are finding her attractive now! She does not need to seize every opportunity for male companionship as if it were the last she will ever receive. She can afford to give herself time.

These middle years are often a period when men are considered to be at their peak. They have reached maturity. A man who has been able to forge a long-term relationship with a woman has an enormous amount of real learning and experience behind him. He, too, can afford to wait before embarking on a new relationship. The stronger he grows the greater the likelihood of success. Anyone who has known real love, friendship and companionship within their first marriage has the right to expect this also in a second. It is worth allowing oneself the time to grow through grief and sadness.

Many men do not wish to embark on a new relationship with a woman and yet they experience sexual frustration and perhaps fears that they are no longer seen as men because they have no woman now to identify their manliness. Some men worry that a long period of abstinence will affect their ability to have intercourse in the future. It is far more likely that problems will grow out of premature sexual relationships, those created at a time of grief and insecurity.

For so many who have lost a beloved lifetime partner, loneliness remains the continuing problem long after the pain of grief has begun to subside a little. The middle-aged man or woman may be part of a system which precludes loneliness, working at an interesting and stimulating occupation which brings them into daily contact with interesting and stimulating people. They may have a wide circle of friends who continue to include them in their lives. They may be part of a caring, sharing, extended family only too eager to go with them on holiday and be there when needed! Anyone whose life is like this has much to be thankful for. They may still feel alone at times for it is not possible to replace that special relationship they had with a partner, but they are the lucky ones. In reality many middle-aged people find that they have only limited access to their family and a high proportion do not work due to health reasons or lack of local employment opportunities. Some may have had to give up their job to care for a sick partner. Many find that couple friends drift away after the loss and that it is hard to create new friendships more in line with their new situation in life. Part of that difficulty in making friends might lie in the fact that it is quite a few years since there was a need to exercise this particular communication skill. Up until their bereavement they had their families. If they did have a problem over the past years it had probably been how to find a moment's peace and quiet in a busy world rather than how to fill long and empty, endlessly unsatisfactory days.

The middle-aged man or woman may feel at a disadvantage for several reasons; because of lack of skills, because their peer group is particularly involved with their own family unit at this time of their life, because they have recently lost their role as parent, one that automatically offers the opportunity of getting to know other parents via school and college PTAs and other child-based activities, and because there may be very little in their local area catering for this specific age group.

Men and women bereaved in their middle years may have experienced, in a relatively short time, great change in the pattern of their life, perhaps moving from being at the centre of their family unit, a position which holds a great deal of power, to being a figure on the outskirts of other groups.

There can be a particular sense of outrage and of theft when widowed at this time. No one expects to be bereaved in these middle years. Some may feel that if they had known their time with their mate was to be so short, they might have done things differently, given more time to their partner, less to an ageing parent who is still alive. In that conflict of interests between partner and growing child they might have made another allegiance. The hard work has been put in, the marriage created, the family raised and supported by the daily grind of a job. Just when the end was in sight, when they looked towards rest and reward, all has been stolen for ever.

Widowed people who have no children often feel themselves to be very different from those who do have children, and of course not all couples have either chosen, or been able, to conceive a child. Childless partners often form very close ties with each other; there is nothing to interrupt their interest in one another. These can be very interdependent relationships and the loss experienced when the partnership is severed by death can appear to be overwhelming for the one left behind.

How does sexuality fit into this picture of deprivation and sadness? It is possible that the drawing together of the couple after child rearing is completed will have created a new era of sexual freedom. Many people find it hard to be relaxed sexually when there are other people in the house, even (or especially) their own children. Alternatively, the tensions and the irregularity of periods associated with the menopause might have been reflected in a barren sexual phase, a temporary cessation of making love, perhaps deeply regretted after the bereavement.

If a man had to care for his sick wife for a long period of time before her death then he will enter his bereavement knowing how to care for himself and for others. It is possible though that he will not have been able to combine caring for his wife with a full-time job. Now he stands alone, minus the partner he loves, minus his work outside the home, and separated from friends and colleagues.

No one who has suffered the death of a partner will escape the necessity to create a new identity for themselves. Part of that process of identification lies in how we see ourselves as men and women, not just as people. Before the death we were someone's husband, someone's wife. Deep inside we may still feel that we are part of that partnership but the world around will be viewing us as single and, in truth, we are alone now.

The widow and the widower who has no partner may find that they are forced to take on some of the skills of their lost partner. They may need to find within themselves the strength, the aggression, the gentleness and patience necessary to survive such a loss. These characteristics do not belong to any one sex but lie deep in all of us. It is not unmanly to nurse a sick wife or to cry, neither is it unfeminine to be strong, to fight for one's rights and assert one's needs. It is in the finding of these different sides of ourselves that we mature, in the very best sense of that word. It is possible that these other sides of our self would never have developed had our partner lived. There would then have been no necessity for us to change and develop with the demands placed upon us.

The middle years are always one of change but never more so than when they contain within them the death of a dearly loved partner.

SENIORITY

Our senior citizens are definitely not expected to be searching for new partners, having fantasies about the opposite sex or doing any of those other things which are generally reserved for the young and single in our society. Even a perfectly innocent remark such as, 'I do miss the company of men since your father died' could be seen as a little risqué. Friends and family forget all too quickly that what has been lost is a member of the opposite sex. To them, a partner may have been a friend or a father or a brother or a colleague. To the widow this was the man she slept with for many years, the person who was her sexual partner for decades, perhaps the father of her children. This was the man who had been in the past, and may well have been right up to the day of the death, a lover.

At the time of writing our society defines seniority as the

point when a woman becomes sixty and a man reaches his sixty-fifth birthday. This is the age when, according to the state, people become senior citizens, able to apply for a state pension and eligible at last for concessions on various travel cards and other perks!

There are few other stages in our life so clearly defined by the date of our birth. After coming of age, at eighteen or twenty-one, our status within society is determined by events rather than the date on our birth certificate. 'Senior citizenship', 'pensioner', 'the elderly', 'old age', each term has its own implications. None is able to convey the vast range of attitudes, feelings, needs and experiences of the millions of people who are amalgamated together simply because they have all reached a certain age.

Because the pattern of family life can be so varied and because life itself is being extended through improved health care, it is possible for a person of sixty plus years to be working, have a teenage child and to be caring for an older parent in their eighties, facing in fact exactly the same stresses and strains of the middle-aged man or woman.

It is also possible for a man of fifty to have accepted early retirement and completed his working life. Children, if there have been any, may all be safely launched into adulthood and he is free to embark on the next stage of his life, that of retirement. In spite of not yet being, in society's eyes, a senior citizen he may feel himself to be more akin to the older generation than his brother who is fifteen years older.

Some people are undoubtedly old beyond their years whilst others seem perpetually young. Anyone who has just suffered a major bereavement may be feeling old whatever their actual age. The pain of grief is so intense, it dominates thoughts and behaviour almost totally in the early months of loss. Bereavement brings us closer to our own death and is a time when we are most likely to contemplate our mortality and question what lies beyond life. Death of someone we love makes philosophers of us all.

However impossible it is to define what we mean by elderly, we can make some generalisations about the special problems and difficulties those in the later years of their life might face after the death of their partner. We can safely assume that the majority of people who are widowed in later years will be losing a long-term partner, someone who may have been part of their life for several decades. Others, a smaller number, will be losing a partner for the second or even third time. A few will have married for the first time late in life.

We can also guess that most elderly people who lose a partner will have retired from their work although many may be involved in less formal or voluntary work. Sometimes it becomes necessary to give up work to care for a sick or ill partner. Sometimes retirement and bereavement coincide with one another within the space of weeks or months. Suddenly the world is a vastly changed and very diminished place.

Most elderly people will continue to live in their own homes by themselves after the death of their husband or wife. Some will move to live with relatives and some will decide to move into a smaller flat, sheltered housing, or a nursing home. Where to live and the upkeep of home and garden can be one of the greatest problems facing the widowed in later life.

Another problem may be that of money. The drop in income faced after the death of a partner can be very hard to adjust to. Most of the household bills remain exactly the same and yet, now, they have to be met on a reduced amount of money. How can a person care properly for him or herself, get out and about, meet new people and join new activities, when the cost of fares is prohibitive and even a new dress or jacket, needed to restore confidence, is simply beyond their means?

Bereavement with its stress and pain and emotional upheaval can seriously undermine health in the early months of loss. This too will affect our ability to get out and connect up with others around us. As we grow older we may find we become more restricted by our health. We may not have the same degree of energy, our eyes may not be quite as sharp, our hearing not quite as acute. It can be hard to separate out the temporary problems due to bereavement from those which are more long lasting. It is all too easy to assume that these feelings last for ever. Well, they don't! The bereaved do not suddenly collapse into senility and ill health. If we had been widowed in our twenties we might have experienced similar loss of concentration and memory. We might have felt low, run down and just as hopeless about the future.

The older we grow the greater our association with death and the dying. We may already have lost our parents, perhaps much loved aunts and uncles, a brother or a sister. It is not unusual for an elderly mother to live through the death of her son or son-in-law. Important friendships are also lost through death. Each beloved person lost will make those that remain more precious and leave us more alone and even less supported. There can come a time when there is no one left alive that knows our history. No one that knew us as a child, or watched us grow through adolescence, that can reminisce with us about what has been before.

Young elderly, the middle-aged elderly and the old elderly, all are just as likely to be facing the same sexual desires and frustrations on the death of a partner as a young widow or widower. We do not cease to be a sexual being just because we reach a certain age. We remain a man or a woman until we die. We are a certain gender and according to the nature of that gender we will react in different ways to others around us just as they will react differently to us.

As a sexual being we may well have sexual feelings; fantasies, desires, hopes and wishes. We may either act upon these or hold them secret, deep inside our minds, perhaps believing that such thoughts are abnormal or that they should have been outgrown long ago. A strange thought. After all, we do not outgrow our capacity to love, to laugh, to be angry or amused. Why then is it expected that this other important side of our very being, one that we were born with, should quite suddenly disappear, leaving us sexless, just because we happen to reach a certain age or lose our partners and have to live on without them there at our side?

It may be that we have no wish to marry again, or to have a sexual relationship with someone, but this is not to say that we are not sexual, that we are not responding at one level as a sexual being. We may note that a man is attractive, that a woman is shapely, we may care about how we present ourselves and how others perceive us. We may care as much about this when we are eighty as when we are eighteen.

Just because we have reached this advanced age, it does not follow that we wish to be segregated from mixed company and encouraged to join predominantly single sex clubs and activities. We may thoroughly enjoy the company of the opposite sex and that undercurrent of pleasant flirtation that it so often contains.

One of the great problems the aged face which does not confront those who are much younger, is the disparity between the number of men and women in this age range. By the age of seventy there just are fewer men than women still around, that is a fact of life, or of death!

For women this means that their chances of being in contact with men of their age or older is lessened. The clubs and activities they join will be mainly female. If they live in sheltered housing that too will be mainly inhabited by other women. If a woman has been used to the company of a man, that of her husband, it can be very hard to be suddenly deprived of this ingredient to her daily life.

One might think that surviving men have no problems! After all, they have the opportunity for female contact all around them. This is true. However, the loss for a man might be the loss of his close friends, of that male group which balanced the female one either within his friendship circle or his family. However much he might like and enjoy the company of women, there may be times when he longs to belong to a male group of his own age again, to be free from the necessity of having to be the only man among women.

Apart from the difficulty of making contact with the opposite sex, if we are elderly we may face those problems created by other people's expectations of what we should be doing and how we should be behaving as an older person. We may find ourselves caught between the need we have for the care and support of those around us and our need for the freedom to explore our future in a way they may not understand.

It is easy for the roles within the family to become reversed after a death; for the parent suddenly to become the child being looked after by their own children. This form of caring support offered in the early days can be so valuable but it is important that it is seen as temporary and that our right to be in control of all our practical and financial affairs is fully recognised. This does not mean that we will not welcome help; someone to come with us to the tax office, someone to help interpret the wording on all those many forms needing attention. But all decisions should, in the end, be made by us. This is our partner who has died, our sadness, our loss and our life which remains to be lived!

Our children have their own sadness, their own lives to be lived. The greatest help they can offer is in the knowledge that they are there, that they care for us and continue to need us as part of their lives. Once we hand responsibility for our future over to our family then it can be hard to take it back again when we need to.

It may not just be the family who attempts to 'parent' an older person and make decisions on their behalf. The doctor, health visitor, home help, or warden may adopt a different attitude to someone they now perceive as an older, grieving person. They may do this for very real and genuine reasons of care and sympathy and they may have valuable professional advice to offer which it would be sensible to follow. However, we must all lead our own lives and there is no one who is more expert on what it is that we need than us.

As we grow older we may find our right to privacy is gradually eroded. Caring children or neighbours may feel it is fine to pop in to check on us at any time, perhaps even letting themselves into our home with a key so that we are not disturbed. The cost of such care can be very high indeed.

If we move into sheltered accommodation, a home for the elderly, a nursing home or hospital, we may find ourselves having to share a bedroom. How can friendships with the opposite sex grow if there is no space, no place for private thought or loving actions? It may be that we will need to overcome our shyness and find the courage to ask for that right to be alone with someone we care for.

If memories of a partner's pain and distress are still fresh in our minds we may be hesitant in making a new beginning with a new partner. Perhaps they too might become ill and need us to nurse them. Perhaps they too will die suddenly leaving us shocked and even more alone. It takes courage to commit ourselves into a new relationship; courage to risk loving once again when we know so well the pain that follows the loss of that love.

It can take time to work out what it is that we need to bring meaning and purpose back into life after our partner's death. We may have to fight for time; time to grieve, time to think before making any major decisions about what we wish to do and where we want to live in the future.

The one thing that the elderly feel that they have very little of is time. This is especially true when they have just lost someone they love deeply and are aware of death and the eventuality of their own ending. In the early days they may even wish that this would come soon, bringing to an end their own pain and loneliness.

None of us can anticipate the years ahead and what lies in them. Although it may feel as if our life on this earth has ended, it may be that we are really just embarking on another stage of our life, that a decade or more lies ahead of us containing experiences that we would never have anticipated in our wildest dreams.

3

Grief

W HEN SOMEONE deeply loved has died those who are left behind will grieve for the loss they have experienced. Although there are general patterns to grief, no two people will grieve in the same way or for the same length of time. Each person grieves in their own unique way for the unique loss they have suffered.

The process of grief is important; it affects how we see the world after a major loss, it affects the way we think and feel and the actions we may decide to take. By understanding grief and its effects we will be better able to understand ourselves.

Rather like a sea, grief possesses powerful tidal currents and undertows. There will be times when these work for us and times when they seem to be taking us far from the safety of the shore. Within the space of a day we will soon discover our own tidal patterns as the sadness within us mounts and diminishes. Each week will hold its unique movement dictated by our personal agenda of events and commitments. Alongside these rapidly discovered regular currents exist the unpredictable high tides that flood in, sweep us off our feet and carry us out to sea. When the current is so strong there is little purpose in wasting precious energy in the struggle to regain firm ground once again beneath our feet. Few are actually drowned in the sea of grief. Eventually, before too long, the tide turns and we find ourself safe on the shore once again, and there we rest, until the next time.

There is no right or wrong way to grieve, there is only grief itself, the slow, gradual journey undertaken by those who have been bereaved. This can start even before the death, when the shortness of time left is realised. It intensifies at the point of death, then moves on through the funeral, that public acknowledgement of the death, and on and on until the time is reached when the bereaved are able to understand and accept the death and the consequences it has had for them personally.

Right from the moment of death the bereaved man or woman is confronted with two tasks and there will be times when these seem to be in direct conflict with one another. There is the need to grieve, often a private, inward looking task, focusing on the present and the past. There is also the need to build a new existence, create structures and routines capable of giving life meaning and purpose once again. This is an outward looking task, one which needs action.

How we grieve will be influenced by several factors. Perhaps the most important of these is the relationship between us and the person we have lost. Each bereavement creates its own set of specific losses and, as we have seen, those following the death of a partner in life are likely to be wide-ranging and last for a very long time.

The more intertwined our life and the life of the person we have lost, the harder it will be to break those many thousands of links that exist between us and them. This has to be done if we are to learn to live on without them now as part of our daily existence. As each knot binding us is broken it creates a fresh sense of pain and sadness. We do not lose someone we love only once, at the time of their death, but again and again.

The whole of the first year of bereavement holds a series of major *first times*. We grieve for the first spring we have to live through without the one we love. How dare the daffodils flower without our partner here to share their beauty! The sense of life and energy generated by a warm spring day only serves to highlight the cold, loveless emptiness of our life as someone who has recently lost their partner. Why have we never realised before that everyone is part of a couple? Everyone is holding someone's hand, sharing a joke together; everyone belongs to someone. Everyone except us.

The sunshine of the first summer alone brings poignant memories of past shared holidays. There is no holiday from grief. Our sadness continues on whether we pack it up and take it with us to the Spanish beaches or simply stay at home. The loneliness is here when we do return from a period away. There is no one waiting for us now; no one interested in hearing where we have been and who said what to whom. We let ourselves into that silent empty place we call our home, unpack the suitcase and get on with life.

The first autumn with its falling leaves and gentle rains can seem to reflect our own sense that everything in life is in the process of ending or decaying. It marks the inevitable passing of time.

Winter brings fears of a different kind. Its shortened days and long dark nights separate us from those around us; those that are fortunate in still having a partner by their side; those who come home to a warm welcome and a shared meal. Those lucky people, only too glad at the end of a working day to pull the curtains tight shut against the cold dark night.

Alongside this remorseless changing of the seasons, the first year of bereavement will hold for each of us its own personal calendar of important events. Family birthdays are now faced alone. The particular pain on reaching 'their' birthday, and our own. For the first time this passes unacknowledged by the one we most want with us. For the first time there will be no special card carrying its special birthday greeting on the mantelpiece. Wedding anniversaries contain so many memories. They link us, year by year, back through time, to the day that marked the beginning of the partnership ended so recently by death. This is an important entry in that private diary of personal loss.

Then there are all those common events that affect the pattern of our lives. The bank holidays which used to provide such a welcome breathing space from the working world may now be days which have to be negotiated with special care. Any occasion previously associated with being together, celebration, shared happiness will, in this first year of loss, cast a shadow of sadness; the greater the significance, the deeper the shadow. Any event which highlights the family, warmth and joy will now emphasise the aloneness of the life of the person who has just lost their partner.

Perhaps none more so, than the first Christmas. 'What shall I do?' 'Can I possibly get through it?' 'Shall I stay at home or go away?' Anxieties over Christmas can start with the first hint of the coming winter. Ultimately, when it arrives, like all other days, it only lasts for a certain number of hours. It is survivable. It is often in the days and weeks preceding a special day that the intensely painful work of grief is done. By the time the day itself arrives we have prepared ourself for it. The first New Year alone may catch us out, following so closely on the heels of Christmas, surprising us with its associated grief and deep sense of loss.

It is through the conquest of each day, each challenge, each new loss that we make our way, often unsteadily, through the first year of our bereavement. There can be a sense of real achievement when we get past that other huge 'first' – the first anniversary of the death itself and see that we are still there, still alive and still coping! Nothing can ever be quite so bad again.

The second year of bereavement can be a hard working one. It is a time when we lay down the foundations for the years ahead and, like all foundation work, that requires a lot of effort and disturbance for what appears to be very little actual result.

Alongside this practical business, the work of grief goes on. There will be longer periods now when we feel stronger, more able to look forward with hope and optimism. But, these will be interlaced with times of great sadness. We are still so close to the huge loss we have suffered, it will not take much to trigger another wave of grief. Just when we felt on top form, just when we were getting our confidence back, we collapse into a nightmare of despair, loneliness and depression. The problem with these periods of deep sadness is that their very intensity destroys our ability to hope. When we are living through such a time it can be impossible to believe that in a week or so we will have passed out from under this black cloud. Some of the middle months of this second year seem to echo the distress of the middle months of the first year. If we know that such low periods are natural and that they pass, it helps us to survive them.

Many people find that it is sometime in the third year following their bereavement that these emotional shifts begin to stabilise. For some, there is an actual happening, a moment in a day, a specific scene, when they feel as if they take a significant step into the future and away from the past. A point when, looking back they are able to say 'that is when I stopped thinking and acting like a bereaved person and became me'. Others find that they go through many such turning points and no one moment stands apart from the rest. Just as we lose someone we love many, many times, so we also make many new beginnings and take many new steps into the future.

The loss suffered when a partner dies can not be contained in any one section of our life. It spills over into everything we do and everywhere we go we are reminded of the past and those happier days when we were living together as husband and wife. The objects around us in our home contain the history of that shared past. We look at the empty chair by the side of the fire, the coat in the cupboard, the ash tray which is no longer used, that special plate that they liked so much and each object creates a contrast between the present and the past. We turn on the television and recognise their favourite programme. We listen to the radio and every spoken word or record played activates a memory. In the early days of loss everything around us triggers the past and a fresh awareness of the loss that we have suffered.

Some people try to protect themselves from such pain and sadness by getting rid of all possible reminders. They clear out the cupboards, empty the drawers, redecorate the living room or even attempt to move right away from the shared home and even from the district they have been living in. Friends and family may applaud such efforts. They see this courageous attempt at a new start as 'a good thing' and sometimes these early new beginnings are successful. Many are not. It is not easy to put down new roots, establish new friendships and create a new life when still deeply grieving for the past. Once the excitement of the move and the thrill of feeling in control of life again has eased away, all too often people find themselves alone, in a strange district, far from known neighbours and friends and longing for the familiarity of the old home.

The opposite of the person who embarks on too much sudden change is the man or woman who wants everything to remain exactly the same as it was before the death happened. The daily routines go on as they did before the death. The shopping is done on the same day, the same food is bought and the freezer and fridge bulge with uneaten goods. Any suggestion that routines for running the home could be even slightly altered is immediately dismissed.

How we mentally let go of the one we have lost is reflected in how we deal with the physical world around us. It is impossible to let go of so much that was so important to us and allow it to slip from our lives. We are human beings and we take a long time to realise fully what it is that we have lost and slowly and gradually to find ways of adjusting to that loss and creating a new life without the one we love.

The process is more complicated than just letting go. It also involves claiming back from the dead things which we see as theirs. This is their chair until the day that we make it our chair and are able to sit in it with ease. This is their side of the bed, their drawers in the dressing table, their half of the wardrobe. Even in a shared and loving partnership, most of us create clearly defined territories which are mutually respected. A wife might hestitate before re-arranging her husband's tools just he may pause before clearing out her desk or the bathroom cabinet.

In many senses, partners belong to one another. We belonged to them just as they belonged to us. In the early days of loss we look in the mirror and say, 'He (or she) would not want to see me like this.' We try to be brave because they were brave. We see ourselves through their eyes. Because they are so much in our thoughts we are very close to the one we have lost at this time, perhaps closer than we have been for years. We do not want to separate from them.

Separation, letting go, claiming back the territory from the dead, all these complex processes take time. Each new day takes us further from the one we have left behind. Each new step into the future is both a success and a betrayal of the past. Learning to say, '*I*' instead of, '*we*' takes a very long time indeed.

Few of us can avoid all sense of guilt as we learn to move forward and let go of our past. We can feel guilty if we think of another man or woman, guilty if we go out with or wish for the company of another man or woman. Even these simple and natural wishes can seem like a betrayal of the one we have lost.

Life partnerships come in many different shapes and forms. The nature of that unique relationship we formed with our partner will affect how we grieve and our ability to create a new life for ourself.

Some partnerships are still very new when they are ended by death, others have lasted many decades. Some partnerships allow both partners the space and freedom to develop and grow. In such unions, outside work, interests and friendships are not seen as threatening to the marriage but are positively encouraged. When a partner of such a relationship dies there will be very deep sadness but the remaining one has a sure base on which to build their future. 'We lived for each other.' 'We never went anywhere apart.' 'We didn't need anyone else in our life.' For the men and women who have dedicated all their love and attention to only one person, the isolation and sense of being absolutely lost and abandoned when that person dies is very great indeed. Sometimes a close bonding is brought about less by choice than necessity. Mental or physical illness can separate out a couple from their friends. Caring for a very sick partner is time consuming and leaves little energy over for relationships and interests outside the home.

In some partnerships there may seem to be one obvious leader and one follower. One partner appears to be in charge, making the decisions, leading the way forward whilst the other may appear to be the more dependent and vulnerable one, either physically, due to health problems or mentally, perhaps because of a past breakdown.

Few relationships are as simple as they appear on the surface. The strong person may draw heavily upon the love and emotional support of what appears to be the more vulnerable one. But over the years patterns of behaviour get built into a partnership and, once established it is hard to shake free from them. If someone is used to seeing themselves as vulnerable and in need of care and attention it is hard to have to take care of themselves. If they have been used to seeing themselves as strong and capable and able to deal with any problem, it can be hard to find themselves swept up in a sea of grief, out of control and frightened.

How do followers survive when there is no one now to lead the way? How do leaders and carers survive when they lose the one they have been looking after? Both will face their own special difficulties as they struggle to rebuild their world as a single person.

Who we have lost is only one of the factors affecting the length and depth of the grief we will experience after a bereavement. *How* the death happens, the circumstances leading up to and surrounding the death, will also play a major part in our ability to understand and accept what has happened and will affect how we learn to live with the consequences of that loss.

There are many ways to die. There are the deaths that follow a long serious illness. There are the deaths due to illness which happen relatively quickly; where there has hardly been time to take in the possibility that the person might die before they do so. There are the deaths which result from tragic accidents when the security of life is suddenly shattered in the space of the moment. Then there are those other sudden, shocking endings due to a heart attack or a stroke. There are the violent deaths, those due to murder or suicide. However a death happens it will leave behind it a special kind of pain and a special kind of grief.

How we grieve will also be affected by the history we bring with us into our bereavement. If this is our first loss then we may move with it into an exploration of our own mortality and the vulnerability of all life. The assumptions of security and continuity that we have held for many years are suddenly threatened.

If our past contains the loss of other important people then we might need to grieve again for all that went from our lives at that time and for the implications of that previous loss as we face this present bereavement. For the first time for many years we may find ourself longing for the mother we lost as a child; if only she were here now, to give us the love and support we need so desperately. If the baby we lost decades ago had lived, then at least we would have their companionship in these bleak days.

Our ability to cope with our grief is altered and changed by the kind of person we perceive ourself to be. Do we see ourself as a strong person, able to cope with adversity and survive chaos and catastrophe? Or, are we a vulnerable person, one that must beware of overstretching him or herself? Have we learned before that we have a great sense of humour? Are we good at making friends? Do we like people and trust them? Do we prefer our own company? Would we define ourself as an introvert or an extravert?

When our identification and sense of self has been shattered by the loss of someone very close to us, we have to find a way of re-identifying ourself. Often we fall back on general characteristics. We cling for dear life to the positive ones, 'thank goodness I have an ability to make friends!' Or, 'at least my health is good!' The negative ones seem like the final straw: 'how can I survive if I am weak or have problems with my nerves or have had a breakdown in the past?'

It is important to hold on to the fact that the death of a partner is a life-changing event. The person we will end up as in the years ahead will be very different from the person we are now. We will have to be if we are to survive.

Our grief will also be moderated to some extent by the support we can draw upon at the time of our loss and in the following months. Knowing that others love us, that we are needed and wanted, helps us to find a reason to go on when the world seems empty and meaningless. Family and friends, a good doctor, an understanding priest or counsellor, a kind neighbour, a caring colleague at work can make all the difference in the world to how we feel.

The support we are offered will, in turn, be affected by

how people see us. If we are known as a person who likes their own company then friends may hesitate before invading our privacy. If we are seen as a great coper, then everyone might expect us to cope without their help. If we are seen as vulnerable, friends may be fearful of coming too close to us, just in case we collapse and make demands upon them that they are incapable of fulfilling.

The length and the depth of the particular grief we experience after the death of our partner will be forged out of a combination of many factors. That special relationship which existed between us and our partner and what it was that we lost when they died will play its part. How they died is also important, whether they were ill before their death, how much time, if any, we had to prepare for that coming end. The help and support we are given, or failed to receive, from those around us. Last but definitely not least, our own unique history that we bring with us from the past into our present period of need.

THE EARLY DAYS

The first reaction to the death of a partner may be one of disbelief followed by a kind of numbed shock. Many people describe this feeling when looking back at the early days of their bereavement. They can remember feeling as if they hardly existed, as if they were a shell, a hollow person, a kind of hurting robot. It was this numbed figure that somehow made the arrangements for the funeral, who found the papers, filled in the necessary forms and took on and completed all those hundred and one tasks which follow the death of a partner. At this time there are likely to be family members and friends close by, offering help. They too, may be feeling shocked and disorientated. They too will be struggling to take in the implications of what has happened, trying to make sense of information which seems almost incomprehensible.

The very early days of bereavement, those which lie between the moment that the news of the death reaches us and the funeral, have a unique intensity to them. As a life ends, a huge task begins. Friends and relatives, the Registrar of Births and Deaths, the funeral director, a religious minister, the DSS, the bank, various organisations, the insurance company and a whole host of other people will all have to be informed of the death.

If we are the partner or next of kin of the person who has died, the arrangements for the burial or cremation of their body will be our responsibility along with the organisation of the funeral service and any gathering that may take place afterwards. A multitude of decisions will have to be made and actions taken and people spoken to, all at a time of deep distress and shock.

The extent of that shock will depend on the circumstances surrounding the death. If a person has been ill for a long time, if he or she was known to have a serious condition, if the death had been predicted by doctors and nursing staff then the impact of the news of the death will be lessened and the sense of shock diminished. Shock may still be present; there is all the difference in the world between some one we love being seriously, even terminally, ill and the fact that they are dead. As long as there is life we can never quite exterminate hope. Death is nearly always a shock.

If the deceased was in great pain or discomfort then we may feel relief that, at last, for them the suffering has ended and that they are at peace. The events preceding the death will have a powerful influence on how we feel in the early days of loss.

If a death comes unexpectedly; the car accident, the heart attack or haemorrhage, through suicide, or even murder, then the shock will be intensified. There has been no warning, no chance at all to make preparation for the prospect of life without that beloved person there as part of it. In a matter of minutes one world has ended we find ourselves existing in the strange and unfamiliar landscape of grief and loneliness.

Grief is not just in our head, in our thoughts and mind; we experience it physically, especially in these very early days of loss. We may find ourselves sighing deeply, feeling sick, having palpitations, head or stomach aches. The pain of grief does not restrict itself to emotional pain but invades the body in the way that is often unfamiliar to us. Our heart can actually ache. Perhaps for the first time we understand that someone really could die of a broken heart.

In the first weeks after a death we may be restless, constantly on the move, shifting from room to room as if we are searching for something or someone. It is at this time that we may sense or feel the presence of the dead person close to us. This might also be the time when dreams or nightmares interrupt sleep.

We are not computers. We cannot programme into our brain the fact of death and press a button marked DELETE that wipes out all reference to the one we have lost. There is no way our very human brain can take in so much change in such a short space of time. Part of us carries on searching even though we know that the death has happened and that the person we have lost is never coming back to us.

The early days of bereavement can be dominated by a sense of being out of control and in many ways we are out of control of ourselves at this time both physically and emotionally. Assumptions we made about ourselves as a person can be abruptly shattered. Before the death we may have seen ourselves as an 'in-command' kind of person, someone who helped others. Now we cannot even help ourselves. We may have felt that we had a good tempered easy-going kind of nature; now we are irritable and bad tempered and feel surges of great anger against our friends, God, the world, our relatives, ourselves and even the person we have lost. 'How dare they do this to us!'

We may have liked to watch television, read books, paint, go for a drive, knit, visit people, listen to records. Now nothing pleases us, everything is pointless and without meaning and purpose.

It can be frightening to feel so much a stranger to oneself. Fear can play a major part in early grief: fear of going mad, fear of being out of control, panic attacks, fear of leaving the home and fear of being in it. We may be frightened of the dark, of dying, of being alone, terrified of the prospect of all those years ahead that must still be lived. We may fear that we are going mad. The death of someone we love, someone who was very important to us, cuts the ground from under our feet and leaves us wide open to all kinds of fears and insecurities in the early days of our bereavement.

Part of the intensely hard work of early grief is the need to look back at the death. It is as if we create a video film of all the important events leading up to and surrounding the death and then run it through in our mind time and time again, searching through the sequences in an attempt to find some order to it, some reason for the death. Perhaps at this time we are also privately searching for that alternative ending, the one in which the death doesn't take place, the one where everyone lives happily ever after.

Sadly it is impossible to change that ending or the events surrounding it. This is the time for if only. 'If only I had noticed how tired she was.' 'If only I had told him how much I cared.' 'If only I hadn't let her drive that night.' 'If only I hadn't slipped out of the room to wash my face.' 'If only I could have been there when she died?' 'If only I had made him visit the doctor.' 'If only the doctor had arrived sooner.' 'If only the hospital could have diagnosed the illness at an earlier date.' 'If only the ambulance had arrived a moment earlier.' 'If only she (or he) was alive now.'

Accompanying these 'if onlys' will be feelings of guilt or anger. We, or someone else, should have been able to prevent the death from taking place, or, if it had to happen, it should have been done better. Few deaths are perfect. Some contain aspects that could have been done better and others, sadly, are very imperfect indeed. With hindsight we see so clearly what could have been improved and we long to have a second chance, an opportunity to travel back in time and put things right. Death does not allow us that chance; unlike any other ending it is forever.

Death draws a line under the sum of our life and, in these early days of bereavement, we are forced to calculate the columns of figures, the pluses and the minuses of the relationship we shared with our partner. Nothing before has prepared us for such a painful task. It is like confronting an accountant who demands that we should have kept every bill we ever received in our life, who calls us to task over the minutest of mistakes. The accountant we have to answer to is ourself. It would be strange if one part of our life, the sexual side should escape interrogation. Few of us could say that we or our partners had been perfect mates over the whole of the time we spent together. There will be regrets but these will pass. Later we will be able to view ourself with greater compassion and more forgiveness, able to view the one we have lost more realistically, acknowledging their strengths and weaknesses alongside our own.

Part of the work of early grief involves this painful searching; this banging of our head against the immovable fact of death. Our eventual acceptance of the huge loss we have suffered is grounded in our acceptance of the fact that we are only human. We, and those around us can neither foresee the future nor undo the past. We can only live, as best we can, in the present.

'I seemed to cope quite well to begin with, but I'm feeling so much worse now.' Unlike an illness we do not gradually recover from bereavement. As the weeks and months pass so we become increasingly aware of what we have lost, our grief accumulates, our sense of loneliness grows. Around the middle months of the first year we may find ourselves stranded on that desolate plateau of hopelessness. The numbing effect of shock has faded, the knowledge of what has gone for ever is within us and we are physically and mentally exhausted from the effort of living through the preceding months.

Even this stage does not last for ever. Almost imperceptibly the pattern of our grief begins to change. Even within the space of each day, patterns begin to emerge. The lowness of the early hours blends into a gradual easing of the pain as we bury ourself in the work of the day. This is followed by a return of the bleak loneliness of the evening hours, often the period of the day we shared most closely with our partner. Quite soon we discover that we have one or two relatively good days when the loss seems almost bearable. These may be followed by some very bad days indeed.

As time passes the better days increase in number. We may even have several of these following one another and begin to feel that perhaps we might just be over the worse. Then another wave of grief knocks us off our feet and it feels as if we are right back at the beginning once again. Of course we are not. Every day we are accomplishing another part of the complex task of accepting that the death has occurred and assimilating its meaning. Every day we learn a little more of the problems involved in living alone without our partner there at our side.

Each of us sets our own time scale for this painful early work of grief. It is a period of intense emotions alternating with no emotions; of tears that seem to drown us or of no tears at all. At such a time all we can do is care for ourselves and take each day as it comes in the sure certainty that it can and will only last for twenty-four hours.

4

Dealing with Feelings

A PARTNER has died. That loss extends into every waking moment of our life. We are grieving for all that has gone from our life for ever. The safety net of marriage has suddenly been withdrawn and we find ourselves alone in the world. At such a time what are our feelings? What do we want most? What is it that we most need?

In these early days of bereavement perhaps all we really want is for the death not to have happened. We want our partner back. If they were sick or had been very ill for a long period leading to the death, then ideally we want them to be, not just alive but well and healthy and by our side once again.

We want to be like our friends, to be an ordinary person living an ordinary life. We do not want to be a bereaved person. Being bereaved means being alone. It means waking each morning to face yet another day, one which now seems to contain nothing except pain and sadness and a multitude of tasks demanding our attention, decisions to be made.

At such a time we may feel that we want to die. What is there now to hold us into life? Life seems now to be comprised of meaningless activities and pointless pursuits. The death of a partner so often takes away all the meaning and purpose of existence for quite a long time.

The frustration of grief is that we cannot have what we want so desperately. We cannot become unbereaved. Death like no other loss is absolute and for ever, at least in terms of life here on earth.

This might be the first time in our life that we have confronted death, perhaps the first time we have wanted something with all our heart and had to face the knowledge that we will never, ever have it. Death presents us with an impenetrable brick wall. We can scream at it, plead with it, hit it with our fists but it will not break down; there are no doors through it to the other side and no way of scaling its height.

Unlike wants, needs are the essentials which are necessary for our survival. We may want to be with people or want to be alone but if our wishes are not granted, if life forces people upon us or separates us from those we love we will probably not die. However, if we do not eat or drink liquid of some kind, if we neglect our health, expose ourselves to the icy winter winds without warm clothes, then we are in actual physical danger. In order to survive at the most basic level we need food and drink and warmth and shelter.

The problem is, if we can't get what we really want and no longer know what we wish for (apart from the impossible) then we may well cease to care for ourselves and begin neglecting those basic needs. This is all too easy to do in the early months of bereavement when the stomach contracts against food; when sleep becomes difficult and we are always tired. At this time of deep grief the sheer effort of survival seems too great; there appears to be so little point in that battle to survive, alone and unloved.

On that bleak plateau of hopelessness in the middle months of the first year, a new wish may emerge; the wish to end all the sadness and the pressures and the pain. This can be especially strong if we believe in life after death and an eventual reunion with our loved one in a future world.

This natural wish of the grieving person to explore the possibility of ending this aloneness is different from the conscious decision made by a seriously depressed person to take their own life. The bereaved person is not a depressive. We may well be depressed but that is reasonable because we are grieving deeply for a great loss. Grief naturally contains these very low periods as well as those better days when life seems almost bearable once again. The wish to start again, to forge a new beginning lies alongside the wish to slip back into the past.

After that initial period of numbing shock, feelings begin to re-emerge. Many of these feelings will be painful, but there are other, more positive feelings, delight in a friend's kindness, amazement at our ability to survive so much loss and cope with such a multitude of problems; a burst of sexual feelings which seems to spring from nowhere.

What can we do with our feelings? We can try and understand them. They are part of us and our grief. In normal circumstances we have a degree of control over our feelings. If we read sad books or watch sad films we tend to end up feeling sadder than we did before. We learn the situations in life that either cheer us up or tend to bring us down. Having said that, we are still capable of being surprised by our feelings which can never be completely controlled.

When we are deeply grieving, our circumstances are not normal, our control system is weakened and we may find ourselves at the mercy of very strong and rapidly changing feelings; anger, fear, intense sadness, guilt or sexual desire. It is perhaps not surprising that in this general out-of-controlness our sexual needs and feelings and desires could also be affected.

'But I've never done anything like that before.' A widow admits shamefully, when confessing that she has gone to bed with her next-door-neighbour, or her best friend's husband, or the electrician, or that nice man from the over-sixties club. Of course she hasn't. She has never lost her husband before, never been so alone, never felt like this before. The very world she inhabits has lost its sense of order. It is not only she who has changed; the people around her treat her differently now. Her neighbour would probably never have approached her in that way when her husband was alive; she would not have needed that lift home then or the electrician in to mend the light fixture. Once the safety net of marriage is torn away the partners who are left are exposed as never before to the world of sexuality.

Those intensely strong emotions of guilt and anger, experienced in the early days of our loss, may also affect our behaviour. If we are feeling angry with ourselves it doesn't matter if we misuse our bodies, sleep around, act in a way that hurts ourselves and perhaps other people as well. The world has let us down. We have let ourselves down. There can be the feeling that we deserve everything we get. After all, we failed in our duty to keep the person we loved alive. Any further hurt and pain we may bring on ourselves is a just punishment and we deserve nothing better.

Why should we care about using others? Why should we worry if we let people down? Nobody cares about us. No one protects us from all this pain and suffering. The world is a hard place and it is everyone for themselves.

The 'merry' widow and widower we read so much about in books can and does exist. When the relationship that contained and bound two people so closely together for many years, suddenly ends, like butterflies emerging from the constricting chrysalis, we may float and flutter from flower to flower. We find ourselves free in a totally new way; free to experiment, to try out different images, different personalities. Free to flirt, free to have affairs. Each new bloom seems to offer more than the last but none really satisfies us. However hard we convince ourselves that we are having a great time, we can't really quite believe it. But, if we stopped flying, folded up our colourful wings, what would happen then? Perhaps the blackness and pain would be unbearable, perhaps it is better to keep moving, perhaps anything is preferable to being alone.

This difficult and restricting period will not last for ever. Even in the very early days of our bereavement we may discover that some things we do help us to block out certain feelings or at least contain them. It probably wouldn't be a good idea to make a conscious attempt to block out all our feelings. Just as physical pain acts as a useful signal that something is going on in our body, so our emotions reflect the hard inner work of adjustment necessary if we are to find a way of coming to terms with the enormous loss we have suffered. A feeling is neither good or bad, it is simply an instinctive reaction to a life event.

Our past, particularly that period leading up to and surrounding, our bereavement will have an influence upon many of the powerful emotions confronted in the early days of loss. The sexual side of our marriage may well have been affected in the weeks, months or even years leading up to a death. A long illness, periods of hospitalisation and severe depression can all deplete the ability, or wish, to make love. Sometimes the wish and ability remain as strong as ever but opportunities to make love diminish for one reason or another. Prior to the death there may already have been quite a long period of enforced abstinence, a time when love and tenderness were expressed purely through the spoken word or caring touch. This contrasts with the situation where making love and intercourse has been a loving, natural, regular part of a relationship, brought to a sudden end by the totally unpredicted death of a partner. Numbness and shock often swallow up all desire and sexual yearning. The loss suffered is so enormous, so incomprehensible that it overwhelms all other feelings. It may be weeks or months before desire returns.

Some bereaved people may experience waves of acute physical yearning in the very early days of their loss. They need now, more than ever to be held and comforted, to touch and be touched. For many people the act of intercourse provides comfort; nothing offers a greater sense of safety and security than the knowledge that they are joined to another living human being. Such feelings so soon after the death of a beloved partner can be uncomfortable. They do not seem to belong alongside grief and yet they exist. Sometimes they dominate all other feelings by their sheer strength and persistence.

The early searching stage of grief may be translated by some bereaved people into a search for an actual replacement for the one they have lost. Something desperately needed has gone from their life and, in their shock and loneliness, it seems logical to attempt to replace it. So a neighbour, a friend or just a kindly stranger becomes the magic cure to all problems. Like the orphan duck that attaches itself to the first moving object it sees, so a widowed person may form a deep attachment to the first available person that appears, however inappropriate.

After such a major bereavement feelings may come and go in a bewildering fashion. Most of our actions, however, remain to some extent, under our control. We may *feel* like giving in our notice at work, selling our home, telling our neighbour exactly what we think of him or her, kicking the cat, but we recognise that it might be sensible to stop and think long and hard before actually *doing* any of those things. Similarly, we may feel sexually frustrated but that does not mean that we have to act on that feeling and immediately embark on a sexual relationship with the next likely person we happen to meet.

Just as we might have to find ways of defusing our anger in the days following the loss of our partner (kicking the pillow and not the cat), so we may also have to find ways of safely defusing our sexual frustration. Some find that physical exercise helps. If our body is exhausted it will collapse the moment it hits the bed and, with luck we will sink into a deep sleep and there will be no opportunity to feel frustrated. Hot baths, cold showers, watching late-night television, putting on the radio, reading a book, getting up and having a warm drink, taking homoeopathic remedies, meditation, yoga exercises – there are many techniques we can try if we feel the sexual tension is getting out of control.

If we have been used to making love it can be hard to deal with the tension and stress that can come from the frustration of enforced abstinence. Of course this is not simply missing the act of intercourse. Making love involves touch, and love, and warmth, and lying closed to someone. Not to be loved, not to have the warmth of a human being breathing in the night at our side; not to be touched in that special way, not to be kissed or to kiss anyone on the lips – this is very real deprivation. A hollowness, an empty place has opened up. This can produce physical symptoms as the body aches and yearns for what it can no longer have, but wants so desperately.

People who have not been used to making love with their partners for a long time, perhaps because of a partner's illness or depression or because the habit of making love vanished many years ago, may be surprised to find that they experience acute sexual desire after the death of their partner. For the first time for many years they feel a physical longing for another human being; an actual ache to be loved and to love.

'Self help, not self abuse!' That is how one widow described masturbation. More men than women admit that they masturbate regularly; however, the number of women prepared to say that they do, increases every year. If a man or woman has never masturbated and has been taught since early childhood that touching themselves *there* is wrong, then no amount of statistics on the subject is going to make them instantly alter their opinion. Habits and inhibitions of a lifetime are not easily broken and some people will never feel comfortable or right about this method of satisfying themselves. We may not have masturbated before simply because there was no need to do so; just as before, there was no need to join an evening class or local clubs; no need to make new friends or learn how to drive, no need to fill in a thousand forms or double lock the back door at night.

When a beloved partner is lost so many new routines have to be developed and new skills learned. Masturbation is a skill. For women, an orgasm is not something which is automatically achieved. We may find that we need to relearn our body, explore the link between the thoughts in our mind and the way we feel. Few people think of nothing when masturbating, most have some kind of fantasy picture. We may be more worried about these thoughts than the actual act, frightened they might get out of hand, worried that they are wrong in some way. As long as they remain contained safely in our mind, they can do us, and those around us, no harm. One of the important aspects of masturbation is that it offers us choice; we can obtain some degree of control over our feelings and desires without having to involve ourselves in outside relationships before we are really ready for them.

Men may feel guilty that their body is so obviously expressing the need for sexual fulfilment at a time when they are grieving deeply for their wife. An erection can seem an untimely and inappropriate physical reaction when our thoughts are full of sadness. It is important to hold on to the fact that we can never be totally in control of our feelings. As human beings a life force runs though all of us and its power can be experienced even after a major bereavement. We cannot prevent it arriving, unannounced and unwanted, but we can choose what we do with it.

We may have become accustomed to the idea that our body belonged to someone else, not to us. When we are children, our parents lay claim to what we can or cannot do with our bodies. Later on, our partner may have strong ideas on what is proper or improper behaviour. This may be the first time we have truly felt that our body actually does belong to us.

What we do in the privacy of the bedroom is our own business. We may wish to talk about it or we may wish to remain silent. Perhaps for the very first time in our life we are truly alone. Because we are alone we are confronting new options, new choices as free adult human beings. That can be very frightening indeed. Remember, only a fine line separates fear from excitement.

THE EMPTY BED

For the man or the woman who has lost their partner, at the end of each long day, there is only the empty bed. There is no one now to cuddle up to; no one to kiss good night. The bereaved partner will have to learn to go to bed alone at night, and wake up in the morning. There is no one now to make love with or be loved by. Never more is the loss of a dearly loved partner experienced than in the intimacy of the bedroom.

We are most open to thoughts and feelings in the quietness of the night. There is nothing now to distract us; no friends calling to see how we are, no work that has to be done, no tasks demanding our attention. All of the defences that help us through the day, slip from us at night.

The large double bed can overwhelm us in its emptiness. Some parents bring a small child into it, perhaps calming two sets of fear and loneliness at the same time. Others prefer to sleep elsewhere in the early nights of their bereavement; in the armchair or on a sofa in another room. Anything is preferable to facing the loss so emphasised by that empty bed. Some brave the bed, but find it helps to fill the vacant side with pillow or cushions or even a giant teddy bear, in an attempt to disguise the gap. Others get rid of the double bed immediately. That side of life is over for ever. They buy a single bed, one that reflects the new single life that they have embarked upon.

Of course many couples choose, for health or comfort reasons to sleep in separate beds. After the death, this leaves a whole bed empty and unused. Should it be kept and used for visitors? Would getting rid of it dispel the loneliness? Is it wrong to act hastily or is any action better than no action at all?

Like many other objects, a bed contains part of the past. If there has been a long period of illness before the death, then sleeping arrangements may have been adapted to suit the needs of the invalid. The bed may have become the very centre of the patient's world. The memories it contains will be ones of the last stage of the patient's life. It may be easier to part with such a bed than the bed which was shared together for many years, perhaps since the beginning of the marriage.

There may be invitations to spend a few days with friends or relatives. Holidays will be taken and other beds in other bedrooms will be slept in, but always alone. One part of life has ended, perhaps for ever.

'Till death do us part' is the contract that most people make when they embark on their partnership. They promise to remain faithful to one another until they are parted by death. It is not a promise that everyone is able to keep but many do and even those who may stray throughout the long history of their partnership often adhere to the spirit of that original contract. When death parts a couple that contract is ended. The process of physical separation begins at the very moment of the death, but mentally many bereaved people feel that they are still closely bonded with the one they have lost for a long time afterwards. It is not unusual to feel closer and more *in love* with a deceased partner when grieving than for many years.

It is in the quiet, dark hours that we have the freedom to explore other, deeper areas of concern. We may still find our thoughts niggling away at the practicalities of daily existence: Have we paid the milkman? Did we answer that last letter from the solicitor? If we made a will should we specify who gets the silver spoons? But space can be made for concentration on more spiritual issues.

Death forces us to question the very purpose of existence. It makes us re-assess our particular role in life and how this relates to the universe as a whole. Many people believe that life, in one form or another, goes on after the physical death of the body on this earth. Some believe that, when they in turn depart this life, they will be re-united with the one that they have lost. Whatever our beliefs they will have an influence on how we grieve and our attitude to new relationships.

How could we love, live with, or marry another person when still in a form of partnership with our first love? If we did remarry then would this new partner also be with us in the life hereafter? If they were, would this create the difficulty of split loyalties between two loves?

It is not unusual to ponder such deep and difficult thoughts in the quiet night hours. Even if we do not believe in eventual union with the deceased we may believe that the dead are still with us in some form or another, perhaps giving precious strength when we most need it, or guiding us through the depths of our loss and sorrow. If they are with us, then what might they think of any new beginnings we might make? Would they be cross if we did get rid of the bed? What about new relationships? Would they understand or disapprove or be angry at our weakness? If our previous partner was a naturally jealous person it is hard to conceive of their tolerating another person in our lives, even after their death. If we promised them before their death, that we would not grieve, that we would find someone else, are they angry at the slowness of our progress? Such thoughts are hard to share with those around who are not bereaved. They can be hard to share with anyone – bereaved or not. They are the kind of thoughts that belong to the night and explode like bubbles in the light of the day.

Perhaps our belief in our God is the only source of comfort to cling to at this painful time. Would that much needed comfort be jeopardised if we explored that darker side to our nature? The anger generated by our loss may become focused on our God. How could he have let such a thing happen? Why did he not answer our prayers? Didn't he hear us when we called out to him? Why should our loved one be allowed to suffer? Why are we suffering? We haven't done anything to deserve this punishment. If he does not care about us, why should we care about him? In our anger the words of prayer freeze on the lips. At a time when comfort from our God and church is most needed, a barrier of doubt separates us from the help we need.

Our bereavement might have forced a re-evaluation of our belief system. This is understandable for it is by questioning that eventually we are able to understand, and through understanding, come to accept. We grow and develop spiritually through this painful process of confrontation and exploration. Most ministers and priests understand this need to question and would welcome an opportunity to help us explore these deep and difficult questions.

If a code of behaviour is based around our religious beliefs, this can come under severe pressure at this time of intense speculation and how we act often stems from our belief in a particular religious code.

Some religions and societies lay down guidelines for behaviour after the death of a spouse; a prescribed period of mourning before they are free to think of a new union. This can be useful as it gives everyone a clear idea of what is expected of a grieving partner. It can be easier to know what we should be doing (even if perhaps we don't actually do it) rather than not know what is expected of us.

For most of us there are few acknowledged rules and the struggle to work out a personal code of what is right and wrong has to be waged over months and even years. It is through such struggles that we develop and grow. The death of a partner cannot and does not leave us unchanged. It forces us to confront aspects of ourselves that would have gone unchallenged had we not lost so much.

Much of the work of speculation and confrontation, of deep thought and painful feelings, of hopes and fears, of dreams and despair, takes place in the quiet night hours as we lie alone in our unshared bed.

WHITE KNIGHTS AND BLACK DAYS

Widows tell tales of white knights that rush to their rescue in the early days of their bereavement; men that bring promises of much needed help; driving lessons, fitting that new lock on the back door, repairing the leaking roof, helping out with the children and mowing the back lawn. Men that carry with them a hidden agenda, the offer of a different kind of help at a time of need.

These are not strangers, these white knights. They may be the husbands of a best friend, the next door neighbour, even a member of the family. How could someone who has been trusted for years proposition a widow in the kitchen within weeks of the death of her husband? The thought is preposterous, unthinkable. People simply don't do that kind of thing. Well, some people do.

Some widows succumb to the wooing of their white knights who promise so much. How could such a thing happen? Quite easily. Death happened. Before they lost their partner they would never have dreamed of doing such a thing. Before the death the thought of wanting someone else, leave alone actually doing anything, might have been unthinkable.

Of course we may deliberately choose to involve ourselves in a sexual affair in the early months of our bereavement and we may even be fortunate enough to find ourselves in a relationship which gives us something we value immensely; something that we will look back upon in years to come and remember with warmth and gratitude. Embarking on a new relationship which contains physical love making can be a solution to sexual frustration. As an adult, no longer part of a pair relationship, we are theoretically free to consider such a course of action. This new relationship might also offer us companionship, comfort and hope at a time when these are so desperately needed.

Some widows and widowers do embark on a series of affairs after the death of their partner; not ready yet for a long-term commitment, they move on as soon as the relationship appears to be getting too serious. Very occasionally a man may fear that if he does not make love for a period of time he will lose the ability to do so. Of course this is not true and relationships based on this kind of testing out are usually unsatisfactory and may create the very impotence that is so feared.

Some people cannot make love unless they feel they are *in love*. If they wish to make love strongly enough they convince themself that this is the real thing. This can work for a while but it is likely to have an unhappy ending. There is a limit to how far we can delude ourself.

There is no perfect solution to the deep loss, sense of abandonment and physical frustration experienced after the death of a beloved partner. That precious, safe opportunity for exploring ourselves and another human being sexually has gone. The world is no longer the safe place it was once.

Now we really are on our own. Of course, that doesn't mean that we will be instantly propositioned by friends and strangers or that we would succumb if such an offer was made, but the fact remains, that we are once again 'on the market', 'fair game', and seen as 'open to offers' and all those other insensitive and unfeeling ways of defining the person who is unattached.

Vulnerable, lonely and desperately in need of being held and loved and touched, if we did make a mistake, slip up and act out of character, it might be shocking but it would not be incomprehensible. The early months of bereavement can be ones of confusion and conflicting desires. New relationships may be entered into quite deliberately.

'I know what I want and I will try and get it!' Or, and this is more likely, they can happen unexpectedly. Suddenly there is another man or woman around. What started out yesterday as a friendship seems to have developed overnight into something totally different. It may not, as yet, include sex but there is the distinct possibility that it could do.

As a newly bereaved partner we may be alone in the world but we are not free of the past and it may take quite a long time before we feel strong enough to embark on new relationships.

The work of grief forces us to look backwards at what we have lost. The work of creating a new existence for ourselves pushes into the future. For a long time we are pulled in opposite directions. There is little wonder that there will be times when we seem to take one step backwards for every forward pace in the spiral of bereavement.

It is wonderful to feel like a woman or a man again – someone capable of being attractive and loved and cared for. Wonderful to have this much needed boost to one's morale at a time when it is most needed. But the new friendships and relationships created at this time are insecure. They grow out of the changing needs of the moment. When we are bereaved we can find it hard to believe ourselves capable of change, hard to believe that we will ever be less needy than we are right now.

In the early months we may have only one clear aim and that is our wish to survive. The decisions we make at this time are often based on quicksilver changes of mood. At one minute we decide that we must have a new home, that it is essential for our survival to put the past behind us and move forward, making a new beginning, a fresh start in a fresh place, far from the pain of the past. Or could it be a new job. Why not throw in the old one? Nothing matters, no one cares and no one understands. It could be a new relationship and with it the wonderful discovery that there is such a thing as love still in a world dominated by death and sadness.

All such new beginnings, based as they are on acute need and deep grief, are potentially hazardous. For a while they offer hope in a world where there is no hope. They pull us towards the future and away from the past. They seem right and logical and we need to feel that we have some control over our lives once more, that we are deserving of a fresh chance of happiness. Of course we are. But we cannot ignore the past for it will not stay locked in the back of our mind. The black days continue. We can not throw the old partnership away as simply as we would clear the wardrobe of unwanted clothes. It will follow us silently into the new home or the new job or the new relationship and wait for us to examine it once more.

If there is one great problem associated with these new relationships created in the early days of our bereavement, it is the fact that most of them will finish. This is not surprising because they are built upon our needs as a grieving person, their roots lie in the shifting sands of grief. What is wanted so desperately today may seem meaningless tomorrow. All too often they bring with them other feelings, especially guilt. They magic us away from the work of grief itself, away from the past with its pain and sadness into the present and the future.

Unless we are exceptionally fortunate in the choice of our lover, we will outgrow them as we develop and change and adapt to our new role and position in life. Some relationships survive these changes, growing with us until they progress into stable and mature commitments. The majority fade away to become part of our past; hopefully a part we will be able to look back on with pleasure.

When they do finish there can be a double sense of loss. There is this new ending, this new loss of all those newly created hopes for the future. Alongside these feelings there may also be a fresh wave of deep sadness as we travel back in time to pick up that work of grief that was put to one side when we moved on ahead of it.

Grief has not been invented by the psychiatrists or psycho-therapists or counsellors. Grief is necessary if we are to become strong enough to take those steps into the future. Through grief we discover ourselves, our strengths and our weaknesses. To lose someone we love, someone we care for deeply, someone who is a very part of our existence, must change us for ever. When the numbing effects of shock have faded, when we have confronted the pain of separation, when we have searched and not found, when we have survived loneliness such as we never dreamed existed and when we have discovered what it is to go through birthdays and holi-days and anniversaries and Christmases and a New Year, all without the person we most long to have and to hold and to share our days with, when we have done all this again and again, when we reach a point when we are less lonely and friendships are based on mutual pleasure and not desper-ate need, then and only then are these new friendships capable of growing into something we can call a mature relationship.

However, before we reach that point we have much to learn. We must venture forth into the unknown, and there is no way we can follow uncharted paths without deviating from the right track at least once or twice. Few men and women who lose a beloved partner travel forward without making the occasional mistake. Knowing one is not quite alone, that many have been there before us and others will be following in our footsteps, makes the journey just a little less frightening.

5

Family and Friends

No man is an Island, entire of itself. (John Donne)

HOWEVER ISOLATED we may be feeling after the death of our partner it is unlikely that we will be totally alone in the world. As the poet John Donne recognised, most of us are connected up to the world around us. The links that join us to our family and friends may be strong or very fragile. They will be altered by the changes we are going through because of the loss we have suffered.

As we take our first tentative steps into our new life, our progress may be closely watched by those who love us. The same hand that we welcome when it reaches out to catch us when we stumble and fall in the early days of our loss, may seem to cling too tightly to us at a later date, when we need freedom to experiment and move forward. The safety net our friends and family created in the early months could restrict us as we grow stronger.

Our friends and family may be a source of delight, support, security or one of aggravation and irritation. The one thing we can not afford to do, is to ignore them and the influence they have in our life.

THE FAMILY

Families can be large or small, extended or nuclear, close knit and passionate or far flung and coolly distant. Whatever the composition of our own special family group the assumption is made, particularly at times of crisis and change, that we belong to our families and they to us.

Our families are important, they contain history. For good or bad they have influenced us throughout the formative years of our childhood and they will go on having some influence on us until the day we die.

The relationships between us and the other family members will be altered by an event as large as the death of our partner. Our need for them will change as will their view of us. Parents, sisters and brothers may continue to be a major source of love and support long after we have technically flown the nest. When tragedy strikes it may be to our close family that we will turn. If the relationship between us and our family ceased to be close many years ago we may be surprised to find that a life crisis brings us once again into close proximity. We may, however, discover that the gap between us and our family increases with illness or bereavement.

Some families cope extraordinarily well when confronted with the need to supply love and support after a bereavement. These same families may find it hard to let go at a later date when the bereaved is ready to fly from the safety of the nest and embark on new, adult relationships once again. Family members, like friends, have to try to find a way of adapting to the huge changes that a major loss brings with it.

Each family group possesses expectations of what constitutes 'proper' behaviour. When a major crisis, such as a death, occurs it is generally expected that other family members will be informed as soon as possible. Some will then go on to play a part in subsequent events. This might be a very small and temporary part – a flying visit to the funeral followed by an annual card at Christmas. It might be a major part, perhaps the offer of a shared home or continuing financial support. It is generally expected that close family members will attend the funeral and be invited back to a meal after the event. They may even feel they have the right to have a say in the planning of the service.

If the partnership which has been ended by death was a new one, the couple very young, or if the relationship was not legalised by marriage, then the family of the deceased, particularly the parents, may assume that responsibility for the funeral arrangements belongs to them rather than the bereaved partner. Much to their dismay, common law partners may find that they have fewer rights than they thought. It is intensely sad if disputes do arise at this time. If relationships have been good in the past it is highly unlikely that things will go wrong now. However, if there have been previous disputes and problems then it is not unusual for these to rise to the surface at a time when everyone is feeling distressed.

The funeral is a rite of passage. It is the public acknowledgement of the death and its importance to all who knew and loved the deceased. Friends, family, colleagues and neighbours, even whole communities join together to mourn the loss and to celebrate the value of the life that has ended. By taking private loss and placing it into the public arena another step is taken on that long journey of acceptance of the loss suffered.

Families may have financial expectations of one another. There may be spoken or unspoken laws that so-and-so will inherit the silver or grandma's bedspread. Such expectations can make the distribution of an estate a sensitive and difficult task. Underlying any claim to an object or to the right to inherit financially is often an emotional claim for recognition of an individual's place in the life of the one who has died.

The untimely death of a young person may place a strain on the system of inheritance. A mother may have willingly allowed the family jewels to pass via her son to his young wife in the expectation that they would in turn be inherited by his children. She may have second thoughts if her son dies and the prospect arises of them disappearing out of the family if his widow remarries.

Second marriages which end in death can create difficulties as children of a first marriage vie with the surviving partner for money or goods. The majority of families deal with the distribution of the estate with sensitivity and understanding. However, if there have been previous tensions and problems it is likely these will resurface at this time.

Many people are affected by the death which takes place within a close knit and caring family. A husband may have lost a wife, parents may have lost a beloved son-in-law. A sister may lose her brother, an uncle – his nephew. Families abide by the hierarchical rules of grief; there is an unspoken acknowledgement that some people will be affected more deeply by the death than others. For example a mother of a son may be the main griever until this role is passed onto the son's wife. Very often this is a true reflection of ties within the family but occasionally a person's grief may be underestimated by the group, perhaps because the relationship that existed between them and the deceased was unclear or unwelcome. A mother who objected to her son's choice of partner and to the fact that they lived together unmarried is unlikely to recognise the woman's claim to grief on the death of her son. Some homosexual partners find themselves excluded from all funeral rites on the death of their partner.

The partnerships created in today's society are different from those of the past. They may contain just as much commitment but many people now choose to live outside a marriage contract, and more marriages are ending in divorce or separation. We are still struggling to lay down structures to accommodate these changes. Should ex-husbands or ex-wives be included in the funeral arrangements? At what point does a love affair turn into a common law partnership?

To some extent, close families tend to apportion the grief within the group. For a while one member will be the strong one, able to support and comfort the others. Later this situation changes and they are able to be supported in turn by those who are now feeling stronger. Men often feel that they should be the strong one, especially in the early days of bereavement and it may be some time before they allow themselves the space they need to cry out their own pain and loss.

Children may find themselves cast as either very vulnerable and hence needing support from a strong parent or, as 'fine' and hardly affected by the death. In reality, all will be coping with their own loss in their own way. A child may well feel that he or she has to be the strong one in a family which seems overwhelmed by grief and it may be a long time before they feel safe enough to reveal their thoughts and feelings. Children are vulnerable because they cannot support themselves. They are dependent on the adults around them and they know it. Their very survival is threatened by the death of one of their parents.

Grief itself cannot be 'shared' with another person but being able to talk openly about the one who has died and accept that each person has their own special pain and sadness can be mutually supportive. In many families this ability to share instinctively the sadness and protect one another provides a solid basis for eventual recovery.

Some family members may have very little knowledge of the needs of a deeply grieving person. They may know that they wish to offer comfort and support, but do not know how best to do this. General statements such as, 'Anything you want, just let us know!' express good will but little else. Older members may feel it their duty to offer the benefit of their wisdom 'Best keep yourself busy, you don't want to dwell on things too much!' What knowledge of grief exists in a family may give a distorted picture of the help thought necessary at such a time, 'Now we are not leaving you alone for one minute, dear. Aunty Enid said she couldn't bear to be alone after her Fred died.' Your needs and those of Aunty Enid may be very different indeed but it can be hard to respond correctly to these obviously well meaning offers of help. To say bluntly that we can't wait for them all to go so that we can just collapse and be ourselves, may be taken in the wrong way and, as anyone with a family knows, it is all too easy for family members to take things in the wrong way.

Many young widowed people are encouraged to return to their parents' home in the days following their loss. There can be great comfort in being 'mothered' again when feeling so hurt and alone. A week or two of being fed, looked after, and cared for, can do wonders at such a time. If there are little children, then knowing that the burden of their care is not resting solely on our shoulders can help enormously.

If the relationship that has been ended by the death was a relatively new one then it can be hard to give up that precious independence, hard to return home as a single person once again. Caring parents may mistakenly feel it would be better if we put the sadness of the past behind us and encourage us to take up our old position in the family as if nothing had happened. At such a time we will need to work hard to hold on to our loss and our feelings and give ourselves the time we need to grieve for all that has gone from our lives for ever.

Families may feel that they have a role to play in guarding a vulnerable, bereaved member against future pain or hurt. This could involve vetting new friendships, advocating caution at all costs. The role of guardian of the weak is not easily relinquished, even when the weak person grows stronger and feels the need to stretch their wings.

Families may also feel that they have an obligation to ensure that a certain level of behaviour is maintained by its members. Bereaved partners are not usually expected to embark on relationships with members of the opposite sex in the early days of their loss. They may have a hard job obtaining the necessary family acceptance for such a liaison even after many months or even years have passed since the death.

FAMILIES-IN-LAW

When a person marries or forms a close connection with a partner they inherit their relations and with them a new set of responsibilities and expectations. The ending of this link in the death of a partner will alter the nature of these important connections. People can choose their friends, but they may never have chosen to share their life with either their family or their in-laws. Although family roles remain forever, the bonds that join in-laws are less well defined and more easily broken.

In-laws can be a tower of strength or a source of continuing additional pain and distress. They are suffering their own personal loss and may be grieving deeply for the beloved son or daughter, brother or sister that has gone from their life for ever. In the early days of their sadness they may feel unable to reach out to another's suffering. Alternatively, in the weeks following the death they may be magnificent. Much will depend on the closeness of the relationships forged before the death.

Children create the necessity for a continuing link between the generations. In some cases, where a closeness has never really been established, there is the unspoken acknowledgement that, if it were not for the children both parties would have let the relationship fade slowly into the past. However, children need their grannies and grandads and their uncles and aunts – especially children already deprived of one of the most important people in their life, a parent. They definitely do not want to lose any more of their precious relatives.

The formation of a new, potentially sexual relationship

may create difficulties between a bereaved partner and his or her deceased partner's family. Parents-in-law can see this as an insult to the memory of the son or daughter they have lost, especially when such new beginnings are made in the relatively early days of bereavement. The widow or widower may find it hard to juggle their own needs for love and companionship with their in-law's need to grieve and their children's needs for an extended and caring family. In some situations it is the in-law family that offers the continuing love and support so valuable to a young bereaved family and, when the time is right, is able to offer support and encouragement to any new relationships created.

CHILDREN

It is not unusual for a widow or widower to find new relationships coming under severe pressure because of the needs and wishes of his or her young family.

Children are capable of great loyalty, generosity, and stubbornness. In their wisdom they may be able to see things that their parent, in the flush of new love, is blind to; or, and this is just as likely, they may be activated by a determination that no one is going to take the place of their dead mother or father. Grief, emotional need and practical self-interest can all contribute to a child's reaction to a single parent's wish to form new relationships with members of the opposite sex.

Children contain their own sexual awareness and their own moral codes. They often have very fixed opinions on the behaviour expected of a parent. Many a middle-aged widow has returned home in the evening after a date to find herself cross-examined by her teenage child. How the young view their parent's actions or inability to act can be determined by their own needs at any particular time, either for security or for greater freedom. A father's courting may be seen as threatening at fourteen but positively encouraged at twenty when the time has come for the young adult to leave home.

Any women expecting a baby at the time of her husband's death can be caught between conflicting emotions. If the pregnancy is in its early days then the first decision she may face is whether or not she feels she should go ahead and have the baby. For some the answer will be a clear, unequivocal, 'Yes, of course!' There could be no question that such a precious gift could be parted with. For others, the situation may be more complex. Babies need love and support and financial security and a roof over their head. In the confused, shocked days of early loss it can be hard to believe that any of these needs could be met. Babies need fathers and this little one will never know the father that created him or her.

The making of such a decision can be further complicated by other people's opinions of what they think the mother should do. The safest advice when shattered by the shock of bereavement, do nothing until you feel stronger, cannot apply in this situation because a decision has to be made quickly. It is important to get expert counselling as soon as possible. Being able to talk through all the possibilities with someone outside the family can help determine the way forward.

The unborn child has no chance to voice his or her wishes. He or she needs nourishment and support to develop healthily. In the safety of their mother's womb they are unaware of the grief and sadness contained in the outside world. They do not yet know that they have lost a father.

Some women are frightened that they will be seen as fat and ugly when they are pregnant; that motherhood will take away their femininity and beauty. Motherhood will change a woman's life for ever but it should not drastically affect her body shape after the baby is born. One has only to look at the screen to see examples of beautiful women who have had babies.

Sexuality and sexual feelings may be the last thing on the

mind of an expectant woman. However, pregnancy is not an automatic destroyer of all sexual desires. In fact some women find that they enjoy the physical side of their marriage enormously, especially in the middle months of pregnancy when it is perfectly safe to have intercourse. Women may have a particularly strong need at this time to be held and touched and stroked. The loss of a dearly loved husband and with him all this affectionate caring kind of love can be hard to bear.

Although some men do find pregnant women unexciting there are others who feel particularly drawn towards the mystery of a woman when she is large with child. A proposition from a man when a woman eight months pregnant might be the last thing she expected but it is not that unusual. Beauty is very much in the eye of the beholder and some men find pregnant women very beautiful indeed. Such a suggestion might seem inappropriate, obscene or merely flattering. How to respond to such an offer is up to the individual and no one else.

The birth of a first child creates a new definition for both partners. They become parents, assuming new roles as mother or father. It can take some time to adjust to these new parts. The newly bereaved widow or widower who has just become a parent has no partner at their side to help them in that new role, no one to share the delights and the anxieties of the early stages of a baby's life. Having just lost the role of husband or wife, they find they have become a single parent. The most important events ever experienced in life, those of birth and death, have been bewilderingly compressed into a short period.

After the birth of her baby the newly widowed mother will need time to grieve, time to heal herself and slowly attempt to bring together those two distinct halves of her life, the past, where she was a wife and the present where she is a mother.

It is not easy to attempt to be both mother and father to

a child. A widowed father may wonder how he will ever be able to give his child the experience of mothering. Will the baby be loved enough? Held enough? Taught all the things a mother teaches a child. Will he have to give up his job to care for his child? A widowed mother may be particularly worried about her little boys. How are they going to cope with having no dad around to teach them the things that fathers teach their sons?

Mothering and fathering are rarely automatic responses. These roles require skills usually learned over a long period. If a woman can learn to mother, then so can a man. Similarly a woman can learn how to supply her son's need for a father! There is no way a bereaved parent will be able to fill all those gaps in their child's life however hard they try, but as they grow stronger, the fears and anxieties of the early days of bereavement begin to fade and their confidence grows in their ability to provide their child with the security it needs. Many thousands of children in Britain are, for one reason or another, being raised in single parent families. They are most definitely not disturbed and depressed children. The vast majority of them are growing up to be healthy, well-adjusted individuals.

Children model themselves on their parents' actions and behaviour and an opportunity to learn about male or female behaviour is lost when a parent dies. But they can success-fully use other role models: the father of their best friend, a favourite teacher at school, an uncle or an aunt! Most children live active, social lives and come into contact with many adult men and women. Single parents may have to make a special effort to ensure that their children join in community activities and have access to other families.

Little children can be helped to build up a picture of their dead parent. They can be shown photographs of them and told stories about the things they did and said. It is not possible for a very young child to hold onto early memories without some kind of re-enforcement. It is important that they realise that because they no longer have a mother or a father it does not mean they never had one. They did have a very real parent who loved them very much.

All of us are born as sexual beings. Little girls can behave embarrassingly like little girls and go through a stage when they are attracted to men, wanting to be cuddled by them, or sit on their lap. If they had a daddy then they would have sat on his lap, but they don't, and so they may look around them for a substitute. Little boys can be fascinated by women, their breasts or their hair or their skin. This is not a sign of disturbance but the natural desire of a child to know more about the world around them which is full of male and female beings.

Some widowed mothers and fathers do not want to marry again or create new relationships with members of the opposite sex. They dedicate their lives to the care and well-being of their children. Other widowed mothers and fathers feel that they have a duty to ensure that they find a replacement parent for their young children as soon as possible.

Perhaps the first duty a bereaved parent has is the duty to ensure their own survival. Children need love and security. They do not necessarily need a replacement parent. A parent's wish to give them one might hide a desire for a replacement partner or fear that they will not be able to cope alone.

Young children are dependent on adults for their survival. The death of a parent will make them vulnerable and that vulnerability is increased when their remaining parent is grieving deeply. But grief does not last for ever and one loving parent can provide all the continuing care a child needs to grow up strong and healthy. This is not to say that a parent must be with their child all the time. He or she will need to learn that other adults and other children exist and learn to accept the rules and limitations of normal life.

Little children are less able to express their sadness, pain or confusion in words. They may show their feelings in their actions, perhaps starting to wet the bed again, or throwing temper tantrums, being withdrawn or particularly clinging for a while. One of the many difficult tasks facing a widowed parent is attempting to differentiate between the normal, naughty behaviour of a child and the behaviour that might have its roots in the loss they have suffered. It isn't easy to know when to be firm and enforce the rules and when to pick the child up and give him or her a big hug!

School age children are verbal and eager to learn. They are exploring the world and trying to work out what makes it tick. It may be when a child starts school that he or she first appreciates that other children have two parents while they only have one. They may put in a plea that this situation, which plainly places them at a disadvantage, should be rapidly remedied.

Explaining that mothers or fathers don't grow on trees, that they have to be just right and chosen with very special care and that quite a lot of children are just like them and only have one parent and get along fine, might help them understand why so little has been done to remedy their deprivation. This is often a good time to talk to the child about the past once again. The death of a parent, however it happened, is a major part of the history of any child and they have a right to that knowledge.

Not all school age children would welcome a new person into the routine and security of their home. The eldest child in the family very often assumes new responsibilities after the death of one of their parents. They might feel that their special place alongside their remaining parent is threatened by an intruder.

The fact that a child is now able to communicate through words does not mean that he or she will be able to express the complex emotions and feelings they may be experiencing. It is important to watch their behaviour closely at home and ask the child's teacher to keep an eye open for any difficulties they may be experiencing at school.

Some newly bereaved mothers and fathers understandably find it hard to leave their children in the care of others. Having lost one precious person they are frightened to risk another loss and hold their children close to them. On the other hand a parent who recognises their children's nervousness will stay close to them until they begin to feel safe once again.

As soon as possible it is worth establishing a routine where we can regularly spend some time each week in the company of other adults. We will want to ensure that the child minder we choose is someone we, and our children, can trust. Ideally a relative or neighbour or the mother of one of our children's friends might be persuaded to look after them for an evening or afternoon. Unless we can afford to pay professional babysitters we face the problem confronted by other single parents, we're unable to reciprocate because we have no partner to watch over our children whilst we babysit theirs. It might be worth thinking of some action or skill we could offer in exchange for baby or childminding.

Friends and relatives might be only too pleased to allow us to go out to the cinema occasionally with a friend, or to a club that they consider good for us, but, and this is a big but, they may not be so willing to look after our children if we are seeing a friend of the opposite sex.

Both our young children and adult friends might need to learn that it is perfectly possible to have a friend of the opposite sex without this necessarily leading to marriage.

It is always worth checking out the secret fears and thoughts of children. They do not always think as we presume they will, and they are capable of drawing very surprising conclusions from the limited facts made available to them. Young children are frequently not given enough information about the important events going on in the world around them. They are left to fill in the missing gaps with fantasies and dreams and this can lead to anxiety and incorrect assumptions.

That decade from ten to twenty contains a vast wealth of change and development as slowly the adult begins to emerge out of the child. This is a backwards and forwards process. No sooner have we, as a parent, begun to feel that our child is on the right road then they seem to slip back again. The death of a parent can affect a child's development. Our children might have to grow up faster than their friends; take on more responsibility and cope with deeper feelings, or, they may need to hold back for a while and take time to deal with their grief before moving forward.

All of us possess three sides: a parent side learned from the parenting we have received, an adult side developed over the years, and a child side. The child is still there inside us and we may be very close to it indeed when we have just lost someone we care for deeply. It is not easy to deal with our children when that needy child inside us is crying out for attention.

One of the areas our children will be busily exploring as they work their way through the minefield of adolescence, is that of their own emerging sexuality. This is not something that can be ignored. Their bodies are openly expressing the changes that are going on within them. It has been said that the average teenage boy thinks about sex once every fourteen minutes. Girls are only slightly different.

It is not easy to deal with this change in our child, especially when the child is of the opposite sex. There is so much talk of sexual abuse nowadays that it is understandable that a father suddenly confronted with his daughter's emerging sexuality should wonder what the right behaviour is. Can we still check that our twelve-year-old daughter has managed to bath herself properly and got the soap out of her hair? Is it OK to give her that cuddle that we know she needs so much? And how and when should she be told about periods and boys, or does she know already? There are so many anxieties and so many questions demanding answers.

Our children will solve a great many of these troublesome situations for us. They will make it quite clear when we are no longer welcome into the bathroom and when they feel too old for cuddles or holding hands in the street. They may be hesitant to bring up the subject of sexuality but there are some excellent books illustrating the facts of life and this can be a good way of opening up a difficult area.

It is never safe to assume that a child knows about birth control. Children often think that they know everything, and talk as if they do, when in fact, the information they hold is sketchy and sometimes downright inaccurate.

Mothers may feel at a loss with their teenage sons as they watch them turn from being a cuddly, little, loving boy into this large distant uncommunicative stranger. Talking with other parents can help enormously. It is through them that we discover that our children are not abnormal and that our parental fears for their future well-being are shared by others struggling with their own teenagers.

Never more than in the early teens are friends of greater importance. What friends think and acceptance by them can be vital, and becoming bereaved, losing a parent can be a threat to the security of our place in the peer group simply because it makes us different from the rest – never a good idea. Children, like adults, can find it hard to know what to say or do with a grieving person and, when in doubt, the basic rule of human behaviour is leave well alone! The last thing a teenager wants is to be left alone by his or her friends.

It is not easy for a child to pursue that normal pattern of conflict and adolescent development when living in a household which is full of sadness and loss. How can they test out their full power against a vulnerable bereaved mother, or a father who is desperately trying to support home and job and children? Children of such homes are often asked to take on more mature roles, to behave well, to grow up more quickly than their more fortunate friends in two parent families. 'If only your father was alive.' A mother despairs at her son. 'Thank goodness your mother's not here to see you dressed like that!' A widowed father sighs as his daughter drifts off into the night. There can be precious little energy left over for the creation of new relationships when engaged in the never-ending battle with teenage children.

How an adolescent will react to their parent forming a new attachment is almost impossible to predict. They may totally ignore the new person, perhaps under the assumption that if they don't acknowledge their existence then they will disappear. They may appear pleased or they may say they are pleased but indicate by their behaviour that they are far from happy about the situation.

A child who has taken a responsible role in the family since the death may be genuinely pleased. They may have been anxious that the burden of care and support they have been carrying might continue indefinitely, perhaps preventing them from going away to college or starting a life of their own.

Alternatively they may feel that all the work they have put into the family so willingly since the death is being swept to one side as this new person enters the scene. They may feel undervalued and unsure of their new position within the family set-up. Many vulnerable single parents form a close partnership with one of their children. Any new partnership will threaten that union and there can be a need for great sensitivity and patience in dealing with such a change within the family structure.

It can be hard for a teenager engaged in the personal task of exploring relationships with the opposite sex; getting involved, falling in love, being hurt, learning to try again, to see their parent at exactly the same stage in life. Is there room in a family for two generations to be involved in the same task at the same time? Some children cope by taking on the role of adult. They assume responsibility for their parent; specifying what time they should come back at night, puzzling over whether or not this new man or woman is the right one. Other children make no secret of their outright hostility towards this unwelcome stranger in their midst. They do everything they can to break up the relationship and few new unions are strong enough to withstand such an onslaught.

As adults, there may be little we can do to prevent this conflict of interests from taking place. If we have been bereaved for a long time, this new relationship; this wonderful, unexpected new beginning may seem to be simply too precious to sacrifice. As time passes and our children grow up, it is possible to envisage a time when they will no longer be with us; when life will be very empty indeed with no partner there at our side, no one to share our days and our nights. Should we sacrifice this chance of happiness, perhaps an opportunity that might never arise again, because our children are reacting so badly? If we decide to fight for our future what damage might we do to our children and their need for security and love?

Our children do not cease to be our children just because they grow up and marry and start families of their own. We remain their parent and they remain our child until we die.

In the early days of bereavement when widows and widowers are so very vulnerable it is not unusual for the family roles to be reversed for a while. Suddenly our children assume control, it is they who are supporting us at this time of crisis and great need. As time passes it is important that this temporary reversal is corrected although there may always be a slight change in the roles because of what has happened. If things are not put right then one can have continuing problems with these older children who assume that, because they have our best wishes at heart, they can control our actions.

[97]

Older children can feel threatened by any hint of sexuality in a parent. Elderly parents, and remember that all parents are seen as elderly to their children, are not supposed to want to go out with members of the opposite sex. They are expected to grow old gracefully!

These older children may have a secret agenda for discouraging an older parent's possible remarriage; after all, it is their inheritance that is being put at risk! However, a child's concern is not necessarily based on self-interest. They may feel genuinely that their parent is in danger of being hurt or of making a mistake that might be regretted deeply at a later date. Their views should be listened to carefully because when one is 'in love' it is almost impossible to see the negative side of the picture. An older child living in the parental home might find it particularly hard to accept such a major change which potentially threatens their position in the family. They may have grown accustomed to seeing the home as their own and of course their position should be carefully considered before taking any action.

It is possible to get caught between our own needs and those of our children. If we are in love, then there will be our new partner's feelings to be considered as well. It takes skill and patience to hold on in the face of such conflicting interests. Whatever our children's age, be they three or fifty-three, their needs will have to be noted and understood, even if ultimately, their wishes for our future are to be overruled by our own needs and desires.

FRIENDS

We may dream of a lover but the reality is that our life in the early months of our bereavement, will be more likely to include friends, neighbours and acquaintances.

It is worth remembering that friends possess other friends and relatives; that each new person we include in our life brings with them their own circle of loved ones. Worth remembering also, that love can grow out of friendship – perhaps with greater success than friendship grows out of love.

Some years ago, a magazine conducted a survey of its widowed readers in an attempt to find out what they felt had been their greatest sources of support in the years following the loss of their partners. Daughters, sons, parents, doctors, counsellors were all mentioned but, right at the top of the list was a good friend.

A friend cares about us. We can talk to a friend. A friend is there when we need them most. We can go out with a friend, chat over a cup of coffee, share secrets, laugh or cry. A best friend stands between us and loneliness. One of the great problems with losing a partner is the fact that, very often, it is our partner who has also been our best friend.

However isolated and lonely we might feel (and many widowed people do feel very isolated at times) few people are totally alone in life. Each of us exists in the centre of our own network of relationships. Although we may rarely calculate the extent of our personal system, we acknowledge that we are fortunate in having our friends and assume that, if ever we needed their help, they would be there, just as we would be there for them, if they needed our support.

Some people are truly alone in life. Beloved relatives or friends have died or are living far away. A necessary move into sheltered housing or a different part of the country has separated them from colleagues and neighbours. The elderly invalid, the widow returning to her homeland after living abroad, the person brought up in care with no family roots are all potentially vulnerable to real aloneness.

For those of us who are more fortunate, never more will we need our friends than after the death of our partner. In the very first days of shock and distress it is often this group of caring people we turn to, and their response can be magnificent. They share with us the sadness of the loss, they are there beside us at the funeral. It is possible to feel enveloped by a community of love, and their offers of continuing support are deeply reassuring; they will always be there if we need them, we have only to call and they will come.

Some of our friends will indeed be there for us – not just in the early weeks of our grief, but months later when we need them even more, and years on when we feel the wish to talk about our sadness once again. They will remain, the strong secure lines that hold us intact at a time when we are most vulnerable. The valuable links between our past, present and future. Sometimes it will feel as if there is nothing but them and their care between us and the empty void which has opened up beneath our feet.

There can be periods in the very early days of bereavement when sheer grief overwhelms all other needs; when it is almost impossible to listen to ordinary people saying ordinary things without wishing to interrupt them and say, 'Did you know my husband has just died?' This stage does pass and it becomes possible to accept that life goes on in spite of the tragedy that has disturbed the very core of our existence.

There can be times when the world seems divided between 'them', those who have never experienced a major bereavement, and us, the sufferers who have first-hand knowledge of death and loss. It can be hard to cross the gap that seems to yawn between the two groups and sometimes, even our best friends are trapped on the other side of the chasm and we are unable to reach them.

We may have to work at keeping our friends after our bereavement. In the early months of loss we are having to test our surroundings constantly. Our emotions change rapidly from optimism to deep depression. We will have many times when we will not know what we want and our friends will be in a similar state of uncertainty. They won't be able to guess at our needs and it is important that we are not afraid to ask for their help. At the same time we should stress that they must let us know if what we ask is inconvenient. They have their own lives to lead and it is important that they do not think we will be offended if a request is refused. Even when we are at the time of our greatest need there may be little things that we can do in return to help them.

Some bereaved people find that they experience a period when they hide away from the world; a time when communication with those around them is just too difficult and it is easier to avoid contact, to stay inside and close and lock the door. The work of grief can force us to look inwards rather than outwards and we need that quiet space to think and to feel and allow ourselves just to be. We do not wish to be cheered up, looked after, cared for, listened to, taken out of ourself or entertained. We want to be alone.

If such a period extends for any length of time it may be necessary occasionally to exercise the basic skills of communication. These, like any other skills, can get rusty if they are not used. If we have been thinking at a very deep level about death, and life after death, it can be hard to relate on a lighter more superficial level. We find it hard to discuss clothes or the greenfly situation, the weather, or a neighbour's quarrel with her daughter, after concentrating purely on ourselves and that personal inner voyage of exploration. We might have to learn to be interested in, or at least act as if we were interested in, what others are saying.

Friendship is a two-way affair. We have to be able to listen to another's troubles, delight in their pleasures and shiver with their fears. Any relationship which is based purely on one person's needs for love and attention, will very quickly run out of steam. Friendship has to be fuelled by common interests. Those founded on mutual pursuits and similar backgrounds flourish, whilst the hothouse relationships of pure need wither when they confront the first frosts of winter. It is never enough simply to want to be wanted in return.

It is impossible to calculate beforehand the extent to which our friendships will be affected by our bereavement. Important relationships may suffer because of our loss. Not only are some people not there when we do pluck up the courage and ask for that proffered help, but we may begin to get the distinct impression that we have become a burden, an encumbrance to our nearest and dearest.

Unwritten and often unspoken contracts underlie all the relationships we form. At one level we know these exist and accept them. Many of the contracts were negotiated years ago and we no longer need to even think about them. We know that if we invited Mrs X we would also include Mr X. We would not dream of sharing a holiday with Y or invite Z to our home unless we also included S. We know that we would go to A if we felt unhappy, that B has a good sense of humour and we would never dream of opening up a political discussion with C or talk about religion with D. Likewise our friends fit us into their pattern of friendships. We fulfil certain needs for them. We may cheer them up or entertain them or be a useful person to have at their dinner table.

Some of our friends will be able to adjust rapidly to our changed circumstances. They will accept that we are not fun to be with in the early days of our loss that for a while we will not be interested in them and their problems. The natural balance of the previous relationship has shifted. As long as we are in a crisis situation it is impossible for us to reach out to them and their needs. We are simply too much in need ourselves.

Most people have very little idea of the after-effects of a major bereavement. They do not understand grief or know how to act towards a grieving person. This is possibly the first time someone close to them has lost someone through death. They can see we are unhappy and because they are our friend they want to make us happy. If we are happy then the friendship can go back to how it was before and everything will be alright once again.

If something is wrong then quite naturally we want to put it right. We all want to find answers and solutions to the situations that cause us unhappiness or discomfort. Some friends will search for ways to make us better. They will come up with suggestions to cure loneliness or solutions to our sadness. If we do not seem to follow their advice then they become dispirited or feel we are not trying hard enough to help ourselves. They may not understand that there is no cure for grief. In the very early days all we may wish for is our loved one back at our side. This is something no friend, however caring they may be, can provide. Friends often feel impotent and helpless in the face of our suffering.

Our friendships may be longstanding, stretching far back into our childhood, others will be formed more recently. Some people will be just 'our' friend, others will belong to us and our partner. It is these last ones, our couple friends, that may be more affected by the change in our circumstances and a surprising number of our friendships may fall into this category. We may have been used to playing cards with one couple on a Wednesday evening, and sharing holidays with another. Although friendship exists between the individuals, the basis of the contract is formed on the group itself. These can be very satisfying friendships indeed but they are vulnerable when one of the four friends is no longer there and the balance of the foursome dwindles to an awkward group of three.

Many of our social events may have been dependent on us being a part of a husband and wife team. Failure to receive an invitation to an evening out, an occasion we would previously have attended with our partner, can be deeply wounding. Discovering we are the only 'single' person at an event can make us feel awkward and out of place. Finding that a 'kind' host or hostess has provided a 'spare' woman to balance our aloneness and disguise our loss may embarrass or anger us.

We may turn up to the gathering and, realising that the

effort to pretend to be happy is beyond us, mumble apologies and slip back home. Next time when we don't get the invitation we are surprised and indignant at our exclusion. If they don't want us we won't want them! It is all too easy for that gap between us and our friends to widen.

Not all the qualities of friendship will be present in each of our friends and it is worth working out what each one might be able to contribute at this difficult time. One may be an excellent listener, another may be practical, providing invaluable help with the completion of forms, another may not like to talk but will enjoy just being with us and by being there bring a breath of fresh air into our life.

A friend in need is a friend indeed! Some people are very good indeed at times of need and crisis; they excel in looking after people in trouble, perhaps they have learned through personal experience what it feels like to lose someone through death. However, these same friends might find it hard to shift gear later on, when we grow stronger. Others are simply hopeless at times of trouble but make excellent good time companions when we feel the need of a laugh and a night out.

If we have been used to being the person who helps other people then it can be hard to take this reversal of roles and our friends may have trouble in getting used to the new, vulnerable us. We may have to keep telling ourselves that this is only a temporary stage, that we have not suddenly become a weak, forgetful, vulnerable person who will have to rely upon the good will of other people for the rest of our lives. We are that same strong person who happens to be going through one of the most difficult and demanding situations known to humankind. In surviving this we will need to draw upon enormous reserves of strength and energy and courage.

There will be times when the love and companionship enjoyed by our friends fortunate in still having their partner will highlight our loss and make us feel even more alone. It is hard to contain our envy as our friends go home to join their partners; hard to listen to them planning trips together. Hard to listen to descriptions of rows between couples and even harder to accept that a marriage partnerships can be ended voluntarily by divorce and separation, that people could actually choose to live alone. However hard it may be to listen to stories of the everyday lives of our friends it is even harder to be excluded from this part of their lives; to be aware that such normal topics have now become taboo in our company because of our loss.

The feelings of a bereaved person towards those around them can change rapidly; 'Everyone is so wonderful, I don't know what I would have done without them'. 'I never knew that people could be so cruel and thoughtless.' 'No one understands unless they have been through what I am going through.' 'I am totally alone. I might as well accept that fact and get on with life.' 'Most people are not all that bad.' 'A lot of people are actually alright once you get to know them.' This wide range of attitudes might be experienced over many months but it is possible to go through the whole list in the space of one difficult afternoon.

Our new position in society means that we might find it helpful to make new friends; perhaps get to know others who, like us have lost a partner. Even if we remain closely bound to our couple friends, we may recognise that, as a single person now, we have a greater need for stimulation and company if we are to fill the long, empty hours previously spent with our partner.

Our old friends may find it hard to accept these new friends. They may feel threatened, feel that we are changing too fast and leaving them behind. They may need to be reassured that we still care for them and need their company and love. Once again it is us who may have to work hard to hold onto these precious friendships from the past, helping them to understand what it means to be us, left alone after being one of a couple.

The recognition that something is missing in our life, that we are feeling isolated and alone can be a sign that we have reached another stage in that long journey through bereavement. The fact that we feel a need to join up with the outside world once again is usually a sure indication that we are growing stronger. We are ready to take yet another step into the future.

NEIGHBOURS

Neighbours can be a source of friendship and support or the cause of irritation and despair. The enforced proximity of the neighbourhood relationship gives it the potential for much good or a great deal of harm. Perhaps it is not surprising that the closer people are forced to live to one another the greater the need for privacy and 'minding their own business'.

It is not unusual for neighbours to remain unaware of the fact that a death has taken place nearby. They may have been away when the event happened and out shopping on the day of the funeral. The knowledge of a death may filter very slowly through a neighbourhood and this can make it hard for the bereaved who may be unsure who knows what has happened and who is still ignorant. The days when a whole community gathered together to partake in the 'wake' have long gone, especially in larger towns and cities.

If neighbours do not mention the death, it may be sensible to bring it into the conversation at the earliest opportunity. Many people find it very hard to open up such a subject. They may wish to offer their condolences but feel it rude to say anything, or be fearful that a wrong word might cause upset or offence.

Even though it would be unfair to expect a previously

neglected neighbour to turn overnight into a miracle of care and compassion, it is worth starting off on the right foot. Now we are alone in life, we are that much more dependent on those around us. Neighbours are a potential source of child minders, feeders of cats, waterers of the garden and minders of the home while we are visiting friends or staying with relatives.

If we live alone it is our neighbour who may be the first to notice if anything did happen to us; if milk wasn't taken in, or newspapers collected from the letter box. It may be they who notice that we appear to be a little low and depressed. They may not do anything but the fact that they are keeping an eye on us, even from a distance is useful.

Of course it may be our neighbours who may become first aware of any new relationships we form. Neighbours can seem to have a sixth sense as far as visitors of the opposite sex are concerned. The news of our loss may have taken some time to circulate in our community but the fact that we had a man or woman in our house late at night can spread like wild fire.

COLLEAGUES AND ACQUAINTANCES

If we work full time we will be spending a large part of our waking hours in the company of our work mates and their response to our sadness, will be of great importance to us.

Because our ability to remember and to concentrate can be affected in the early months of grief we may be particularly dependent on our colleagues' goodwill during that time. Some bereaved people find their work a place of refuge when they are grieving. The routine of going to the same place at the same time each day gives a sense of structure to a world which has precious little to it any longer. The very demands of the job can force painful thoughts to the back of the mind, and for a while, there is the illusion of normality.

Our acquaintances may include the people we see regularly at church or our local religious meeting place, or those who attend the same clubs or activities as us. They smile at us and seem pleased to see us but they do not know us very well or we them. It is possible that these acquaintances will prove to be a potential source of new friendships. Before we lost our partner we had no need for these relationships to be extended. Now our circumstances have changed, even if an acquaintance remains just that, they are still important, they are a means of exchanging a greeting, a smile, a word of communication with another human being.

6

Making a New Start

ONCE UPON A TIME, a long time ago, we used to be part of a couple, a partnership of two people. Now we are alone, we look back on that good time and think of everything that has gone from our life; the humour, the feeling of being attractive, the touching and sharing, the skills of loving which are now obsolete, the pleasure and the passion. It is with a start of surprise that we realise that, not only are we missing our particular man or woman, we are also missing that special contact with a member of the opposite sex which was part of our life for so long.

This thought can be disturbing when it first appears. This is an out-of-character and unfamiliar us. How could we, who perhaps only a year ago were devastated with grief, be thinking now of accepting other people into our life? When this idea first arises many people hurriedly put it to one side. It is an uncomfortable thought and it seems better to dismiss it as an aberration, something best not talked about – a bad feeling!

If the thought arises in the early days of grief and sadness then there might be some sense in containing it, although it is still not in any way, bad. It is a natural reaction, a recognition of one aspect of the loss we have suffered. We recognise that the death of a partner might bring financial loss or the loss of a driver or the loss of the person who cooked and cleaned for us, so it is also natural to recognise that the death of a partner brings to an end a physical relationship which may or may not have included the act of sexual intercourse. It may also have seriously affected the proportion of time we spend with members of the opposite sex.

Whilst the newly bereaved person might search for a replacement mate, a housekeeper, a female companion, a love, the new start we are contemplating now, is not based on the need for comfort which some seek in those sexual relationships formed in the early days following the death; the desperate search for solace and peace and pleasure when all around there is only blackness and despair. This new start is taking place at a time when we are beginning to feel whole again, at least most of the time. When the waves of grief and deep sadness come less frequently. When we are able to look back at the past months and years and say with a degree of pride that we had indeed done well, not just to survive the seemingly unsurvivable but to have learnt how to live alone and think alone and stand alone on our own two feet. This new strong person that is us stands up, looks around and makes a conscious decision that something is missing in life and that specific something is contact with an attractive man or woman.

There is all the difference in the world between identifying what we want and finding a way of acquiring it. To those who are safe within a family group, or contained securely within a mixed network, the thought that it could be hard to meet another man or woman might appear ridiculous! After all, men or women are all around us – in the buses, on the streets, sitting in cafes. Wherever you look you can see large numbers of men and women. What could possibly be so hard about meeting and getting to know a few, reasonably suitable, potential companions of the requisite sex?

Anyone who has seriously set about the task of trying to meet such a person will tell you that it is far more difficult than anyone would imagine, we are far more selective than we think. We select by age, usually seeking someone in quite a tight age band. Men often tend to look at women slightly below their own age, women slightly above. This presents the older woman with an immediate problem because there are less men than women in the later decades. We usually favour a certain type of person; someone from a similar background, approximately the same class, someone whose history is a little like ours. We may not think of ourselves as 'fussy', but could a non-smoker, live with a very heavy smoker or, could someone who is teetotal live with someone who likes nothing better than a night out at the pub? And it would be so much better if their belief system was the same as ours. Could we learn to love their collection of grass snakes? Does it matter that they hate jazz?

In some small isolated towns and villages there may seem to be virtually no selection at all. Every man or woman over puberty is either married, attached to someone else or is absolutely out of the question for one reason or another. How can a new start be made when there is no one there to make a new start with?

Even in large cities the front doors do not readily yield up a suitable list of potential suitors. Just as it is possible to feel most alone in a crowd, so the task of finding one unattached, single, likeable man or woman can appear totally impossible in spite of being virtually surrounded by members of the human race.

Widows all too quickly find themselves tightly contained in an all female circle – the Women's Institute, the Church Circle, the Over-Sixties Club – the older they are the harder it can be to meet unattached males. That is a fact of life. Widows of all ages find that women friends are happy to see them alone but that they are gradually excluded from the couple events.

Even widows and widowers who are at work have their problems. Not all jobs automatically bring them into daily contact with eligible and fanciable free spirits. Any advances that are made are usually from the well and truly attached; the spouse of one's best friend or a married work colleague.

Proper new starts are best embarked upon with others who are themselves free to begin again. It is not always easy to define the extent of that freedom. 'I am waiting for my divorce to be finalised.' 'We separated years ago.' 'We only live together for the sake of the children.' 'We are just good friends.' 'My wife doesn't understand me.' 'He doesn't mind if I see other men.' With so many people choosing to live together outside marriage it is harder to define the importance of existing partnerships. Undoubtedly more marriages do end now in divorce but does that mean that our potential lover will end his or her marriage and be free to give us the love and commitment we need?

If we have been used to being either wife or husband to our partner, it is very hard to be demoted to the role of lover or mistress. We are not used to being a 'secret', to having to share the love of our partner with another person, a person who may have a greater right to it than us. We have never been fitted in to someone's life before: the late evening visit, the brief afternoon meeting, the fear of what the neighbours might think. Illicit love affairs contain a high degree of emotional and physical excitement. If we do embark on such an affair we need to know that we are strong enough to cope with all the complex feelings it will generate in us; the doubts and uncertainties, the guilt and rationalisation, the fears and the anguish, the consequences of our actions. Few people are completely free of obligations once they reach the middle years of their life but some are much freer than others!

This might be the point to think seriously about the nature of the relationship we are looking for. Marriage might have been the only option when we entered our previous union, but we have moved on since that time and our personal circumstances and the world around us have both changed. If our childbearing years are over, if we have responsibilities to existing children and family members, the union we are searching for now, may be very different indeed to the one we established with our first partner. The relationships we choose to form now will be based on the fact that we are a mature, adult, responsible human being.

We are free and we are still looking for that Mr or Mrs Right. Where do we start? So many people, describing their husband or wife will talk of them as their best friend. It is possible that this friendship grew and developed over the years of the marriage but it is also likely that the marriage survived because it was based on the fact that the two people were friends before they married; besides loving one another they also liked one another.

This being so it would seem logical that the person we may eventually wish to be part of our new start in life should also be our friend. It is even a possibility that they might already exist as part of our present circle of friends. It is well worth having a good look at all our friends and their friends and brothers and uncles and second cousins. Is there anyone there who we might be interested in getting to know a little better? If there is, we would already have a headstart, a mutual connection, a thread already running between our life and theirs.

If no likely candidates spring to mind it is time to move on. The next step is to increase our circle of same sex friends. This may seem illogical. We already have quite enough friends of our own sex it is the other sex we are interested in now. That is true, but it is worth bearing in mind that friends come complete with their own circle of friends and relatives. The more people we know the richer our social life becomes, the greater our chance of being asked out, the higher the odds that we will meet interesting people. This is an excellent plan for life which may or may not eventually yield a potential new start companion.

It is also worth looking long and hard at the male/female ratio of the activities we already belong to. If, as a man we find ourselves perpetually in the company of other men, down at the pub, at the club or on the bowling green, it might be sensible to investigate other local activities. Similarly, as a woman, if our life is dominated by all female companionship then we too might think of joining other groups which present a more balanced membership.

Most towns and villages have far more happening than is first apparent from a superficial glance. When we were part of a couple, there was no need for us to research our area activities and clubs. In the first months of our bereavement we may have made several abortive attempts to get out and meet new people. At that time we were grieving and needy, now we are stronger. What failed to work for us then may well prove to be far more successful now. It is well worth giving the world a second chance. We have little to lose and much to gain.

Most towns have political parties and these are usually reasonably mixed groups of people only too keen to welcome new members to their midst. Local adult education colleges offer a wide range of courses. Men may like to consider the embroidery and cookery classes. Women might find the car maintenance and woodwork classes invaluable. Then there are the rambling clubs, the local history societies, the choirs and music groups, there are bridge, whist and bingo gatherings, local church or religious centres, voluntary societies, health clubs, the list may be unexpectedly comprehensive.

If we are totally disinterested in local history, stamp collecting or classical music then it is worth avoiding these particular activities. But, before we condemn them for ever, are we absolutely sure they hold no interest for us? After all, this is a new start we are talking about. A new start needs a new us. Of course a totally new us is impossible, but it is possible that, perhaps for the first time ever, we have the time and opportunity to investigate ourselves. When we were young we may never have had the chance to explore history or stamp collecting or classical music. Usually our likes and dislikes are based on a mixture of influence from outside and luck in what actually reaches us. Now we have both time and the opportunity. After a few meetings we may find that we were right all along, that we do not like history or classical music, but stamp collecting, well, that holds real possibilities and it just happens to be run by a rather interesting person!

Information about local activities can be obtained from the library, the local Citizen's Advice Bureau, the local newspaper and from the people around us. Don't be afraid to ask!

Solo and singles clubs abound. Few local newspapers fail to contain details of at least one such group for the over-fifties or the under-forties, the age range varies but most welcome new members to their ranks, especially unattached men. To qualify for the term single or solo a person should be unmarried. Such clubs may contain a mixture of unmarried people; the widowed, those who are divorced and some who have never married. Those who are separated from a partner are not technically single but might turn up as there can be a long lonely period while awaiting the finalisation of a divorce.

It is worth remembering that a person can be technically single and yet still be very attached to someone. The bereaved can be far from ready to form new relationships in the early days of their loss. Divorced people may also be still deeply attached to an ex-partner, either by love or by anger. The last thing anyone wants to become is a third party in a battle between warring ex-partners.

We may feel it safe to assume that an unmarried man or woman is free to embark on a new meaningful relationship. Technically they may be unattached, but it may be worth exploring why someone as nice as that is still free at their particular time of life. Some people assume responsibility for an aged mother or father or a sick relative which prevents them from forming long-term commitments. Are these relatives still around and, if so, what makes us think that we will succeed where others failed? Some people take a very long time to grow up. Their charm allows them to form new relationships but the demands they put on these soon place them under threat. We would need to look carefully at someone's history which contained a multitude of short-term unhappy love affairs.

Some people have very little history; no family or friends that we can meet, no one that knows them from the past, no links by letter to relatives abroad. Such a person might be someone whose life has contained great loss or much movement and travel. They might, however, be someone who has a history which they do not feel able to share with us or with anyone else.

If we know that someone's history contains violent actions or periods of mental breakdown we are better able to make decisions about the future. Such knowledge does not necessarily preclude a closer relationship. We, too, are bringing our history with us which may also be far from perfect. It would, however, be unwise to dismiss the implications of such knowledge out of hand.

Dating and marriage bureau schemes need to be approached with caution. This is a route best taken when all else has failed. In order to survive the hopes and let-downs, the highs and lows a person needs nerves of steel, common sense and a well developed sense of humour. Some people have succeeded in meeting future spouses or lovers through such schemes and there is no reason why we should not be one of the lucky ones. At the very least we may have adventures and encounter situations outside our normal experiences. By joining such a scheme we should be aware that we are entering the marketplace. Friendship, marriage, introduction and dating schemes are mostly run by people as a business. Such businesses thrive because in today's complex society people find it hard to get to know one another and for a multitude of reasons are willing to approach a third party and pay them a sum of money, in exchange for which, they will be introduced to other people who also wish to get to know someone. 'What am I looking for?' This is the first question we must have clear in our mind. Are we looking for a friend of the requisite sex? Or a lover? Or a potential life partner? 'What am I prepared to offer?' When entering such a scheme we should have a clear picture of ourselves, who we are, what we want and what we have to offer those who will be meeting us.

There are a variety of schemes putting men and women in touch with one another. Some will be concentrating purely on relationships which are intended to end in marriage, others in friendship. They will charge a variety of fees and offer a variety of services. It is important to remember that older women statistically outnumber older men and will therefore be in competition with other older women for the remaining males. Any agency which fails to mention this simple fact of life may be after the money only and not give much in return. Contracts are very important and it is unwise to hand over any money or sign any contract with an agency unless the terms are fully understood.

The agency may promise a certain number of contacts with suitable men or women for a certain sum within a specified time. We will need to know what they mean by suitable and whether or not this is the same as our meaning of suitability. There are other questions to be answered: 'How far am I willing to travel to meet these suitable suitors?' 'What age range am I specifying?' 'Does the agency have a clear picture of the kind of person I am searching for? If not, is that my fault? Have I failed to be specific because of shyness or ignorance?' Some bureaux work on the principle of no marriage, no fee. They may interview each client personally but are more likely to take on only those people they feel they can place.

Computer dating schemes offer the prospect of wider

choice and it is easy to get carried away when looking at the pictures of happy couples, hand in hand who have, so the advertisement tells us, met one another through that particular dating scheme. Undoubtedly people do meet one another in this way and undoubtedly a percentage will end up married. It is impossible to say in advance if we will be one of those lucky ones. In exchange for a sum of money a questionnaire is completed by all the clients. These details will be fed into the computer which will then produce a list of reasonably compatible people within reasonable reach of each other. Candidates will not be personally interviewed and there will be few safeguards to weed out the unstable, neurotic or downright peculiar. It is up to us to read the details carefully and proceed with caution.

An alternative method of getting to know other women and men is to place an advertisement or to respond to one, local papers sometimes carry lonely hearts columns.

If you feel strong enough to embark on this journey into the unknown it is still good common sense to take precautions and remember that, as a single person you are vulnerable. Not everyone you come in contact with will want what you want or behave as you do. For safety's sake: if corresponding use a box number, try to retain anonymity until it feels safe enough to reveal a name. If forced to give a name to someone you are not sure of yet, use just a first name for identification purposes. When establishing the next point of contact preferably take their telephone number rather than giving them your own. Never arrange a first meeting at your home or at that of the person you are to meet. Use a safe public place, such as a cafe, a station or a pub. If they are obviously not right be prepared to say so at the beginning of the relationship. They are more likely to be angry if they feel they have been led on only to be dropped at a later date. Remember that the normal rules of friendship do not apply when using dating services. It is sensible to pay your own way on initial dates, whatever the pressure to be treated. This way there is no obligation and there can be no misunderstanding about who owes who what. Don't be persuaded to do something just because everyone else is said to be doing it. Be prepared to fight for your own moral standard. If they do not like what you are or what you are prepared to do, or not do, then they are free to leave.

It is worth researching opportunities for advertising before taking the plunge. A local paper or notice board might have the advantage of attracting local people but there is always the possibility that someone already known might reply. Of course, this need not be a disaster! Such local advertisements are relatively cheap to place. If courage fails you can always opt out at the last minute and not follow up any responses that come from the advertisement.

It is sensible to read other advertisements carefully before placing one. It is important to attract the right kind of attention from the right kind of people. An advertisement should not be so vague as to receive a response from everyone from eighteen to eighty, nor so concise and detailed as to be impossible to fulfil. Quite a few journals and specialist magazines run friendship schemes. These can be free or cost very little and may be worth investigating.

If we are housebound through disability or ill health, or live many miles from local habitation then it might be worth exploring the various pen friend schemes that exist. This can be an inexpensive way of forming a friendship. It is possible to grow very close to someone whom we may never meet face to face. As thoughts and feelings tumble onto the paper, the differences that may have precluded friendship in the real world, slip away.

Some people find that looking for a future partner becomes an end in itself. In the search for one companion they discover a new and adventurous side to their personality which they never knew existed. We may encounter such people on our travels. They are usually charming, caring companions, thoroughly appreciative of our company but they are likely to have many other friends and lovers and be unlikely ever to exchange this way of living for the confines of a faithful marriage.

Of course it is also possible that we might also become such a person! Once the new start begins who knows where it might lead us?

NEW RELATIONSHIPS

'Would you like to go to the cinema next week?' 'We could have a drink together one evening.' Or a meal or a coffee or a dance or a night on the town. That's how new relationships begin, with the offer of another meeting. Two people have met and one of the them has decided that it would be nice to meet again. If that meeting is a success then there will be another one and another and suddenly they find themselves slap bang in the middle of a new relationship.

The two situations which spin us most wildly out of control are losing someone we love and falling in love. Anyone who has lost someone they love through death will understand the power of bereavement. They know what it is to think of someone night and day, longing for their presence, going over and over in their mind everything that they did together, reliving the past time and time again. Anyone who has suffered a major bereavement has personal experience of the pain and the emotional upheaval such a loss brings with it.

Perhaps bereavement allows us to experience the passion of being in love once again. Temporarily it changes that solid love we had for our partner into a form of idealisation. The pain lies in the knowledge that it is a love that can never again be realised. Death has denied for ever our ability to touch or be with that particular person. The greater our awareness of this fact the more intense our longing for them becomes.

These highly emotional and disturbing feelings do not last for ever. They have an ending and when it comes the loneliness and emptiness which follows them can be hard to bear. Now there is no love, no passion and precious little hope that such emotions will ever be experienced again.

Little wonder that when we do feel the first stirring of anticipation it comes as such a shock and has such an effect upon us. In vain do we tell ourselves this is just a friendship. No friendship gave us this feeling in the pit of the stomach. No friendship required us to take half an hour in front of the mirror before going out or encouraged us to spend money we could ill afford on a new outfit. This is no friendship; this is love. More accurately we have fallen in love and it may be many years since we last felt as we do now.

Falling in love is very different from loving someone. Love is a steady constant commitment to another human being. Being in love is primarily physical. This is not to say that we have to touch someone to be in love – teenagers are in love with their pop idols – but the effect of love upon us is experienced physically. Such reactions are outside our control and being out of control can make us feel uncomfortable.

When we are in love we wish to see the person again. We think of them constantly, we are not ourselves, at least not the self we have grown used to over the years. Suddenly our logic system is disturbed and we see life in a different way. The things that were most important to us yesterday no longer matter in quite the same way. What really matters now, is the person we love and our ability to be with that person and come closer to them. We may be subject to swiftly changing mood swings – those high and lows so characteristic of being in love. We may find ourselves singing out loud, or suddenly weeping. Being in love is waiting for the telephone to ring, not quite knowing what clothes to wear. Being in love is feeling like an adolescent again. This is understandable because most of us will have done most of our falling in love during our teens and early twenties. The feeling may be much the same but of course our life circumstances are greatly changed. The first difference between then and now is the fact that we are older and we have a longer and more complex history behind us. The person we are in love with will also have their own history.

The second difference is that it is possible that we will be the only person who is 'in love' that we know. Unlike the young, we may have no peer group to share our experiences with, no friends willing to listen to all our hopes and fears for the future. On the contrary, our friends may have us neatly categorised as widow or widower, as a poor single person. They may find this new role we have assumed as 'person in love' very hard to take.

The third difference is that now we have no family behind us making those rules which gave us security when we most needed it. We may still have parents but there is a difference between a young girl telling her boyfriend – no she can't be out late because her parents will be furious, and a fifty-year-old man pleading the same excuse. Our children, if we have dependent children, can play a similar role. 'I have to be back for the baby sitter', and 'my little one is such a light sleeper' can offer similar protection from pressure to move forward too rapidly. If we have no elderly parents in need of attention or dependent children then we are on our own. There is only the truth to fall back on, 'I don't want you to come in tonight!' or, 'I need more time'.

Of course we may not need more time. We may feel that this precious opportunity is not to be wasted, that the only thing to do is to grasp the present and live it to the full. When we are in love it is not just the demands from the one we love that may be disconcerting, we may also discover a powerful inner force and find ourselves caught in a personal battle as one half of us advises caution but the other urges us onwards.

Our friends and family may attempt to advise us but ultimately the responsibility for our actions rests with ourselves. We are adults and, as such, capable of making decisions. In retrospect these decisions may seem a little flawed. We may look back and wish we had been less cautious or alternatively be bewildered by the mistakes we appear to have made. However, none of us possesses the ability to look into the future. All we can do is live our lives the best we can.

Falling in love is not restricted to the young or to the single and technically available. It is possible to fall in love with totally unsuitable people. This may not be the first time we have faced such a situation, we may have done so before, either before our marriage or during it. The ability to be bewitched lies dormant in all human beings. It is not something we necessarily go in search of, it is there within us, capable of being triggered into life at any time.

If we no longer have a partner then there is no reason why we should not be free to fall in love again and, having fallen in love go on to create new long-term loving relationships with other men or women. Although we may be free in theory to move forward we may find, to our surprise, that something is holding us back. Logically we may know that it is years since our partner died, we know that we have grieved deeply for them and for the ending of that part of our life. We may have consciously made the decision to start again, make new relationships, believing that we are ready for this move into the future.

Months, perhaps even years have passed since our bereavement. We are ready to begin again yet, when we meet someone we find our minds turning back to the past. We find ourselves comparing this newcomer to that beloved person we have lost and we find our new man or woman wanting. Or, even worse we find qualities in them that our previous partner never possessed.

It is easy to slip into remorse and guilt. Any movement we make into the future seems to carry us away from the past and that can bring with it a fresh wave of grief. For a while we are caught once again between the demands of the past and the wish to create a new life for ourself. We may need time to explore these difficult feelings, they too, are part of the work of grief. They will not last for ever.

Some people feel guilty because they seem to be replacing their dead partner by this new person who has entered their life. Of course we can never replace the one who has gone. They will always have a special place in our lives and in our thoughts. They were unique and the qualities they possessed were unique. This new man or woman will bring their own unique qualities with them into our life.

Although a certain amount of guilt is perfectly natural at the start of any new relationship it is worth taking the time to try to understand the reason for its existence. In what ways do we feel guilty? Why should this feeling arise at this particular time? Sometimes such feelings dissipate when examined. If they refuse to go away then perhaps we are breaking a personal code of behaviour. The rules of society may be far from clear at such a time and we may be uncertain where our own boundary lines exist. If our behaviour makes us uneasy and unhappy over a period of time then it may be wise to give ourself a breathing space, withdraw for a while and see what effect that has on how we feel.

For some people disquiet will be moderated by the knowledge that their deceased partner wanted them to find someone else. It is not unusual for someone who knows that they are dying to discuss the future with their husband or wife and give them permission to move on at the right time. Many people are parted from their partner with no opportunity for such discussion. If our partner was a particularly possessive person we may know in our heart of hearts that they would definitely not have given permission for an involvement with another man or woman. It is not easy to work out what rights the dead have over our lives. They are denied the opportunity to change their minds, to develop with altered events. We who are left behind have to change if we are to survive in a drastically altered and diminished world. At a certain point we may need to give ourselves that permission to move forward into the next stage of our life.

The new person we are proposing to take into our lives will possess their own qualities; their failings and their delights, their irritating ways and their gifts and skills. It is impossible not to make comparisons between them and the one we have lost, especially in the early days of the relationship. If we are still in that 'in love' stage it may not be possible to focus on the negatives. Even those attributes which may prove irritating in the future will be seen as part of their fascination and character at this time. Just as we may have idealised our dead partner after their death so we may idealise this new beloved person that has entered our life. Whether caused by death or love, idealisation does not last. In time we are able to focus more clearly on the true strengths and vulnerability of those we are close to.

Not everyone falls in love. Some learn to love slowly and gradually. Out of the close friendship develops a more intimate relationship. This may grow without us being aware of it. One day we find that we feel deeply for this other person in our life, so deeply that it has become almost impossible to imagine a future without them there as part of it.

What are the rules of courtship in our present day society? Reading certain newspapers we might be led into thinking that nowadays just about anything goes. This is a gross over simplification of reality. Although a very wide range of sexual behaviour exists which stretches from promiscuity to total abstention from sex outside the marriage union, most people live their lives according to their own personal moral code. Occasionally, for a variety of reasons – love, deprivation, anger or even revenge, this is broken.

It is possible that this is the first time we have been in a courting situation for a very long time. We may feel trapped between our own wishes, our friends and family's need for us to act in a certain way, and the demands placed upon us by our new love. In desperation we may search for a set of rules which would simplify the situation.

Our memory will take us back to that courtship that took place between us and our partner and the rules we either adhered to, or broke, in those days. This may produce a standard which seems a little old-fashioned in today's world. Undoubtedly things have moved on over the past decades. This is not to say that we have to move on with them and necessarily adjust our standards to those of modern civilisation. Each of us has the right to draw up our own personal boundary lines of behaviour and stick to them. It is important not to be bullied into taking actions which cause us anxiety. A relationship which is grounded in love and trust will allow for space for both partners to grow and develop within it.

Perhaps the only true rule is that which is equally applicable to every area of life; to attempt to take no action which sets out to cause damage either to ourselves or to other people.

As we grow older it is all too easy to forget that the primary function of intercourse is the reproduction of the human race. It is vital that we never make the assumption that it is safe to make love. There is long period in a woman's life when she may still be fertile even if her periods appear to have ceased. The stress of bereavement can throw the monthly cycle into confusion for quite a long time. It is a gesture of responsibility and care to ensure that every precaution is taken to prevent an unwanted child.

Making love is an immensely personal and physical act. We expose ourselves to another human being in a unique way. Just by taking all our clothes off and standing naked in front of someone else we become very vulnerable indeed. We need to feel safe if such an act is not to cause us concern and fear. Our partner too, has to be assured of our goodwill. We and they need to be treated with dignity. We need to know that the language we use, the private vocabulary of sex, will not be ridiculed, that our actions will not be misin terpreted or discussed thoughtlessly with friends at a later date.

We need assurance that the person we make love with, would not willingly expose us to any harm; that they would tell us of any disease they had that we might possibly catch from them. The fear of Aids has tended to over shadow our concern about all the other sexually transmitted diseases but they still exist.

If we have not reached a point in the relationship when we are able to discuss such fears then it is a sure sign that the relationship is not yet ready to contain the act of intercourse.

Both partners in a new relationship will bring with them a ready-made history. We know our own past; it contains the death of our previous partner but that is only one part of our history. The person we are now is a product of everything that has ever happened to us since we were born. How we think and act is a result of the parenting we had as a small child, the relationships we have created and the happiness and sadness we have encountered. All this we carry with us into this new relationship.

So too, the man or woman with whom we are entering this new relationship brings with him or her, a rich history of events. Perhaps they too lost a partner by death. This may have been the starting point, the common factor that drew two lonely people together in the first place. Their bereavement may have occurred many years ago or be very recent indeed. If the latter, then they may need time to grieve before committing themselves to a long-term contract. We may have to hold on to that golden rule: do not make any major life changing decisions in the first year of bereavement. Of course, rules are made to be broken but a basically good relationship will grow if we give the time and the space to do so.

Our potential partner may be single because they have lost their partner through divorce. This is a different form of loss and one which we, as a bereaved partner, will have to work hard to understand. Sometimes the break up of a marriage will be amicable, both partners choosing to go their own way, perhaps remaining on excellent terms. Sadly, many marriages end acrimoniously. A divorce can create anger and the sense of having been victimised by the other, 'bad' partner. Children and property can all become wrapped up in the disputes that arise at such a time. It is important that the intense feelings created by such a painful situation are recognised and worked through for it is not easy to live with someone who is seeing the world in such black and white terms. We may be the good one at the moment but, it is all too easy to slip into that bad role vacated by the ex-partner.

Perhaps our potential partner has never married. They may have been living in a marriage-type relationship but have felt unhappy and frustrated by its terms. Maybe events in their life have conspired to keep them single, perhaps the care of a sick relative or the heavy demands of a particular job.

Because our past is such an important factor in creating the person we now are, it is worth taking time to explore one another's background. As mature adults we need to know what we are taking on. If we are aware that our potential partner has had previous mental breakdowns then we will be prepared if they become ill again. If we know they have a financial commitment to an ex-partner or children from their first marriage or an elderly aunt in America, then we can take that into account when planning our budget. Likewise they have a right to information about us; our health, our income, our phobias, our family, our fears as well as our dreams.

Not all new relationships will end in marriage. Some will remain as friendships, some as loving partnerships outside marriage. Others will explode causing pain, anguish and regret. Each new relationship rapidly creates its own history. It has a beginning, an established middle ground, and sometimes, sadly it will have an ending.

For anyone who has suffered a major bereavement all other endings must trigger back some of the pain of the past. We grieve not only for the lost hopes bound up in this new relationship which has ended, but also for all the other losses we have experienced.

When we enter new relationships we expose ourselves to the possibility of further loss and pain. If we love we have to accept that the loss of that love will cause us deep sadness. The alternative is to hold ourselves apart from all deep involvement for ever; a high price indeed to pay for peace of mind.

PLANNING FOR THE FUTURE

The new relationship has been established. A fortunate couple have met and fallen in love and decided to marry. Like an ending to a stage play the curtain comes down, the cast bow, the audience applauds and then departs content in the knowledge that the starring couple will live happily ever after.

Of course there is a very real chance that they will live happily ever after. However, there is sadly the possibility that the relationship will flounder and fail for second marriages have a higher break-up rate than first ones. Such an important event as our whole future should not be left to chance or fate. Relationships, like anything else of great importance that we create in our life, demand attention and skilled care if they are to thrive. It is sensible that as much as possible of the preparation and groundwork for the union is done before the actual marriage ceremony rather than after it.

Not all couples opt for marriage. Some will decide to live together; if so, there will still be questions which will need serious consideration. Where should the home be? Will the household include dependent relatives? What financial arrangements should be made? What security is being offered to both partners?

Relationships may be forged out of mutual need and love but their survival depends on clearly made contracts. It may seem inappropriate to speak of contract making when one is in love and busy creating an atmosphere of mutual trust and respect. Never is it more appropriate. Young couples coming together for the first time bring very little in the way of property and past relationships with them. If a young couple renting an apartment and having no children, find themselves separating, there will be pain, sadness and anger and some causes for potential dispute over who has what, but probably both will be free to move on, earn more money, rent another room.

This is a very different situation to a widow who has two main assets, her home and her widows benefit. Her benefit will end on her marriage or decision to cohabit and that leaves only her home. If this was to be lost she would have no chance of earning enough to replace it.

Men and women entering new partnership agreements need to think very carefully indeed about their future security if anything were to go wrong in the relationship, or if their partner was to die. They may also need to consider protecting their children's right of inheritance. These are matters that should be raised before any contract is entered into. Both potential partners should consult their solicitor and take their advice. A will can be drawn up in advance of a marriage which will offer some protection and security to all concerned in the event of death.

There may be an obvious place to set up home but even this should be explored thoroughly before being accepted as the only possible way forward. Economic sense may have to be weighed against other factors, closeness to an ailing parent, a child's need for continuity of schooling, leaving behind close neighbours or good friends.

More wars have been fought over territory than anything else. There is not a species on this planet which is not, in one way or another, defensive of its territory, that space that it controls by right of ownership. Men and women are definitely no exception to this rule. In the first flush of love we may be able to live quite happily anywhere with our partner but very soon we will find that we need to define our territory and the rights we have over the space we inhabit. If there has been a long period of living alone then it may be even harder to learn to share space with another human being. We grow accustomed to being in sole charge of what goes where in the home.

Ideally couples should begin their new partnership in new premises. Neither will have presumed rights over the territory and there will be no ghosts from the past to haunt the union; no proper way to place a table because that was the way the deceased partner always used to do it. By the time we are ready to create a new partnership we should have completed that task of claiming back the territory from the one who has died. There will always be objects and places associated closely with them, but we will be in charge of our environment, able to shift and change it at will, able to move from it, if necessary.

However, we do not live in an ideal world and it may be sensible for one partner to move into the home of the other. This situation requires great tact and patience on both sides. It would be thoughtless for the newcomer to arrive intent on stamping their mark on every single room immediately. It would also be insensitive of the owner not to respect the wish of the newcomer to make some minor changes in the home; after all, this is now half their home too. If it is to be a properly shared home both partners must have a mutual say on decisions made about it.

It would be remarkable if two people's taste did absolutely coincide over everything from design to decoration and tidiness. After a period of being alone it can be hard to learn to adjust to someone else's pace of life – can it really take someone an hour to have a bath and wash their hair? If we are always early for an appointment, how are we going to adjust to the person who is always late? If our idea of housekeeping is a whip round with the duster when the sun shines, our prospective partner might be in for quite a shock.

Money may not be the root of all evil but it definitely plays a potential part in marital conflict. Relationships are inextricably tied up with money and it is worth taking this fact on board right from the very beginning. There are many different ways of sharing a family budget. We may choose to have a joint account or opt to keep individual accounts or go for a combination of the two, thus giving an opportunity to pool some resources whilst maintaining a degree of independence. Who is responsible for paying which bills needs to be discussed. Obviously any system which places the burden for these on one partner and frees the other to buy the luxuries would not seem fair in the long run. Financial obligations for continuing support to elderly relatives or children should also be talked through right at the beginning so that the bill for granny's private hospital or John's down payment on his flat doesn't come as too much of a surprise to the other partner.

By the time most of us have reached our middle years we will have developed our own particular pattern of spending. This may have been tolerated over the years by our previous partner, a period of living on our own will have allowed us the freedom to spend our money very much as we wish, within reason. For some people buying books is essential to their well being and no amount of pointing towards the library will make them change their ways. For others clothes are a high priority, or an annual holiday abroad, rare plants for the garden, or the very best food for a beloved pet! We will need to adapt to another's ways just as they will need to adapt to our own peculiarities.

When men and women who live alone list their reasons for wishing to join up with a new partner, sex itself is rarely at the top of the list. The main reason is often loneliness; the need for companionship, for company and touch. They may also want to be made to feel attractive, to have someone to share their life with, someone to talk things over with at the end of the day, someone to cook for, someone to care for, and someone to care for them in return. If the need for a sexual partner is stated this may be more likely to be by a man than a woman, perhaps because it is still harder for women to express their sexual desires openly or perhaps men are more aware of this side of themselves.

It would be unfair to our future partner if the subject of sex was not thoroughly discussed before embarking on a long-term commitment. During the courtship period this will have been explored but in the anxiety to fulfil all those other needs of love and companionship it can be easy to overlook this very basic desire; to tuck it under the carpet if it looks like presenting any difficulties and hope that everything will come out alright on the night.

Of course, it may do but, equally, it may not. If our ideal marriage includes everything bar the actual act of intercourse then this definitely needs to be stated. Alternatively, if we have been used to a highly active sex life, but have been containing our feelings up to now in the expectation of them being met after the marriage date, we had better sit down with our future husband or wife and talk out with them what they mean by a sexual partnership.

Over the years we build up a pattern of behaviour that suits us best, we create sexual norms, actions we see as right and others we feel to be wrong. There can be a wide range of behaviour in making love. Oral sex is a perfectly normal part of many couples' lovemaking; others might find it distasteful. Likewise mutual masturbation or having the light on, or walking about in the nude. Nervousness can affect how we make love. A shy man may not be able to have or hold an erection. Fear can make a woman feel tight and dry. It can take time and a great deal of patience for a couple to learn each other sexually; to discover what pleases the other and what creates tension and nervousness.

As we grow older many little irritating health problems can make lovemaking more difficult. It may be so long since lovemaking last took place that it has ceased to have any real significance. It is all too easy for the elderly themselves to fall into the trap of thinking that sexual desires diminish with age. They may do for some but they most definitely do not for others.

This can be an area which is difficult to discuss and one where we might have very little opportunity for advice and support from friends. If we anticipate there might be difficulties in our sexual relationship then it is sensible to seek expert advice either from a doctor or a counsellor; quite a few now specialise in sexual difficulties.

Few of us have no family at all. Most of us have some relatives and many of us belong to close and caring family groups. A marriage or the establishment of a new partnership will create interest within our family, and possibly many other feelings as well. These can range from delight to distress, from amazement to acute anxiety on our behalf. Younger family members might find it hard to understand why a parent should wish to remarry at their advanced age. Why not be content to be good friends? The idea of a parent wishing physical closeness or even sexual intercourse may not enter a son or daughter's head.

If the time and trouble is taken to introduce our new partner carefully to our family and ensure that we are properly introduced to theirs a basis for a good relationship will be established. We might need to be patient with those family members who find it hard to accept this new situation. Children used to being seen as head of the family may find it especially hard to take in this stranger threatening to disturb their position. If our new partner is divorced, children from the first union may be living with, or in touch with, their other parent and take on some of their anger and jealousy of this new beginning which seems to have been created out of their unhappiness.

It may be impossible to love all our new partner's family immediately and unrealistic to expect them to accept us with no hesitation. All we can do is act with sensitivity in what can be a delicate area and work hard to ensure that our rights within the family are acknowledged.

We have decided where to live, talked with our solicitor about legal rights of inheritance. We have worked out how much we will have to live on and who will be responsible for which bills. We have talked over where we will sleep and what each of us expects from the other sexually. We have met each other's immediate family and survived the experience. We still love one another and wish to go ahead with a lasting commitment. Ahead of us there are only those minor details of planning to be considered; the when, and the where, and the how, that next step into the future is to be taken. One part of our journey is completed; ahead of us lies the rest of our life.

COMPLETING THE CIRCLE

Three short words – wife, widow, woman – describe the stages that a woman journeys through when she loses her husband; three words that neatly summarise a complex process of changing roles and identification.

To be a wife is to have a clear identity, one which carries

respect and a degree of status in our society. On the death of her husband she becomes a widow, a word that carries connotations of poverty as well as sadness with its images of black clothes and mourning, although, somewhere, right at the edge of our picture, we occasionally catch a fleeting glimpse of a merry widow dancing. As a wife she was defined in relationship to her man and, as widow, she was seen primarily as a person who has lost a man through death. It is only in the third definition, woman, that what she is, and who she is, has no bearing on anyone else at all.

Husband, widower, man are the equivalent words defining the journey a man makes through the period of loss of his wife. He too is firstly defined in terms of the nature of the connection between himself and his wife, first alive and then in relation to her death. It is only in that third stage that he stands defined purely as a man.

Some men and women never marry, their definition remains that of man or woman. Others marry, but are fortunate, their partners do not die. Others become widowed but never move on to reach that third definition of woman or man. After the death of their partner they remain forever defined by the loss they have suffered. Some societies affix the word widow before a woman's name as we might use Mrs or Miss thus creating a situation where it is impossible to escape from that role even if she wished to do so. Other bereaved people choose to remain in the role of widow or widower. They continue to grieve and mourn their loss, unable or unwilling to move forward, reluctant to take that step into the future.

When we reach the third stage, when we become woman or man, we define ourselves once again as sexual beings. This has nothing to do with whether or not we might wish to engage in affairs or be sexually active. It is a mark of maturation, the point when we are able to say: 'I belong to myself and to the present.'

Some who have lost a partner by death will move further

on to find new partners and to assume the identity as wife or husband once again. For them the circle completes itself. Many will not take that final step. Perhaps the opportunity to do so fails to arise, perhaps they make a conscious decision not to marry again. Many people living on their own, discover that their lives hold richness of meaning and purpose, they have no necessity to look for this in the creation of a single permanent relationship with a new partner.

As mature men and women, we may look back at the past and feel regret and sadness for the losses we have incurred, but we are also able to accept the importance of the present, that precious today in which we actually exist which has a worth outside that which has gone or that which is still to come.

As for the future, who knows what the future will contain? In the bleak early days of grief the future was either blank or seen as a continuation of the pain and bleakness of grief. Years later we may be no nearer to defining the future but we have learned a great deal about ourselves and those around us. We possess the knowledge gained from our battle to survive.

A philosopher once said that people divided into two groups; when confronted with a glass which contains some water there will be those who describe it as half empty, the pessimists, and those who delight because it is still half full.

We may choose to define our lives after the death of our partner as half empty, or reach a point when we delight because there is still so much left to do. Whether that entails new relationships, new partners, or remaining alone but going out and buying the biggest, the most beautiful king-size bed we can find, just for us, perhaps does not matter.

Life is unpredictable and so are we. Whoever we are and whatever we may have chosen to do, today is still the first day of the rest of our life. In that sense every day of our life is a new beginning.